SOCIOLOGY OF EDUCATION SERIES
Aaron M. Pallas, Series Editor

Comprehensive Reform for Urban High Schools:
A Talent Development Approach
NETTIE E. LEGTERS, ROBERT BALFANZ, WILL J. JORDAN, AND JAMES M. MCPARTLAND

School Kids/Street Kids:
Identity Development in Latino Students
NILDA FLORES-GONZÁLEZ

Manufacturing Hope and Despair:
The School and Kin Support Networks of U.S.-Mexican Youth
RICARDO D. STANTON-SALAZAR

Restructuring High Schools for Equity and Excellence:
What Works
VALERIE LEE with JULIA SMITH

Finding One's Place:
Teaching Styles and Peer Relations in Diverse Classrooms
STEPHEN PLANK

PreMed: Who Makes It and Why
MARY ANN MAGUIRE

Tracking Inequality:
Stratification and Mobility in American High Schools
SAMUEL ROUNDFIELD LUCAS

Working for Equity in Heterogeneous Classrooms:
Sociological Theory in Practice
Edited by ELIZABETH G. COHEN and RACHEL A. LOTAN

Who Chooses? Who Loses?
Culture, Institutions, and the Unequal Effects of School Choice
Edited by BRUCE FULLER and RICHARD F. ELMORE
with GARY ORFIELD

Hosting Newcomers:
Structuring Educational Opportunities for Immigrant Children
ROBERT A. DENTLER and ANNE L. HAFNER

Mandating Academic Excellence:
High School Responses to State Curriculum Reform
BRUCE WILSON and GRETCHEN ROSSMAN

From the Series Editor

The origins of American sociology of education lie in essays written in the 1920s and 1930s that relate sociology to practical school problems. These works had a strong normative tone, describing what must be done to build character in schools, to achieve academic excellence for all, and to maintain our unique American heritage. Over the ensuing seven decades, however, sociologists of education turned their attentions elsewhere, most notably to fundamental questions of socialization and stratification. Others willingly stepped up to the bully pulpit to preach about washing away the sins of American education. But Americans are no longer such a trusting people. We strive to hold public institutions accountable, and we demand evidence of performance that extends beyond slogans and anecdotes. Comprehensive whole-school reform is a strategy for improving the performance of American schools in educating *all* American children and youth, and not just the few lucky enough to be born into families of privilege. This book is the story of a promising model for reforming the comprehensive high school in the United States: the Talent Development model.

In *Comprehensive Reform for Urban High Schools: A Talent Development Approach,* Nettie Legters and her collaborators blend sociological theory and practical lessons learned, yielding a vivid portrait of the successes and failures of comprehensive whole-school reform.

The most remarkable feature of this story is the evidence that the Talent Development model can transform the culture of a high school, sparking a high level of excitement and engagement among faculty and students alike. Educators can learn from the authors' account of how this change evolved, and from their judgments about what must occur to sustain the reforms. Education researchers can absorb important lessons about straddling the worlds of theory and of practice. We can all take comfort that serious scholars have turned their energies to such an important problem, and that they are committed to subjecting their findings to critical scrutiny.

Aaron M. Pallas

Comprehensive Reform for Urban High Schools

A Talent Development Approach

Nettie E. Legters
Robert Balfanz
Will J. Jordan
James M. McPartland

Teachers College, Columbia University
New York and London

Published by Teachers College Press, 1234 Amsterdam Avenue, New York, NY 10027

This study was supported by grant(s) from the Office of Educational Research and Improvement (OERI), U.S. Department of Education (R-117-40005). The content or opinions expressed herein do not necessarily reflect the views of the Department of Education or any other agency of the U.S. Government.

Library of Congress Cataloging-in-Publication Data

Comprehensive reform for urban high schools : a talent developmental approach / Nettie E. Legters . . . [et al.].
p. cm. — (Sociology of education series)
Includes bibliographical references (p.) and index.
ISBN 0-8077-4225-2 (paper) — ISBN 0-8077-4226-0 (cloth)
1. Urban high schools—United States. 2. Education, Urban—United States. 3. School improvement programs—United States. I. Legters, Nettie E. II. Sociology of education series (New York, N.Y.)

LC5131 .C593 2002
373.12′07—dc21 2001060381

ISBN 0-8077-4225-2 (paper)
ISBN 0-8077-4226-0 (cloth)

Printed on acid-free paper

Manufactured in the United States of America

09 08 07 06 05 04 03 02 8 7 6 5 4 3 2 1

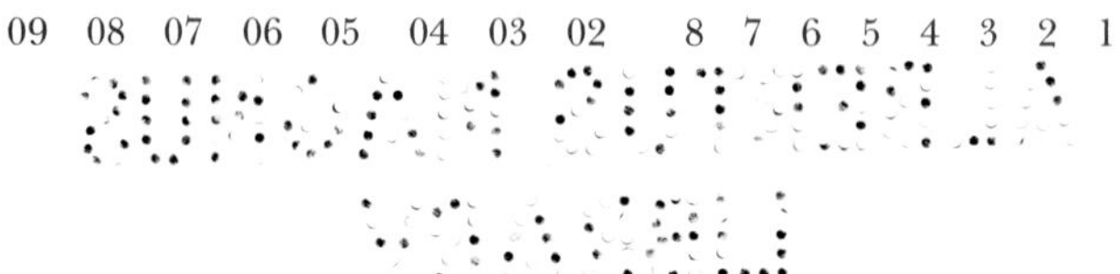

Contents

Foreword by Michael Cohen vii
Acknowledgments ix

PART I What Must (and Can) Be Done: Restructuring Urban High Schools

CHAPTER 1 Introduction: The Challenge 3
A Historical Divide in Secondary Education 6
The Urban Challenge 10
Purpose and Plan of the Book 14

CHAPTER 2 The Talent Development Response 17
Problems and Corresponding Solutions 18
Putting It Together: The Talent Development Approach 27
From Lists to Vision to Action 39

PART II Whole-School High School Restructuring in Baltimore

CHAPTER 3 Context and Planning for Reform 43
Impact of Economic and Demographic Change on Baltimore Public Schools 43
State and District Responses 45
Reconstitution 46
Restructuring Patterson High School: The Planning Year 48
Conclusion 59

CHAPTER 4 "This Is a Real School Now": Effects of Talent Development Reforms at Patterson High School 61
Expectations for Change 61
Research Design 64
Effects of the Reforms 65
Summing Up 77

PART III Challenges to Creating Talent Development High Schools

CHAPTER 5 The Devil's in the Details: Lessons Learned from Implementing Talent Development High School Reforms 81
Unexpected Implementation Hurdles at Patterson 81
Emerging Divisions in Year 2 87
Lessons from Patterson 92
Sustaining Reform at Patterson 96
Conclusion 98

CHAPTER 6 The Story Continues: Early Scale-Up Efforts in Baltimore and Philadelphia 100
Initial Scale-Up in Baltimore 101
Lessons Learned from Early Scale-Up in Baltimore 102
Early Work in Philadelphia 106
Sustaining Reform in Baltimore 109
Conclusion 113

CHAPTER 7 Lessons Applied: Replicating and Extending the Talent Development High School Model in Philadelphia 114
A Revised Planning Process 114
Impact on School Climate and Attendance 117
Moving Reform into the Classroom: The TDHS Ninth Grade Instructional Program 122
Conclusion 132

CHAPTER 8 Hope for the Future of Comprehensive High School Reform 134
Perspectives on the Future of American High Schools 135
Re-Energizing the Movement for Urban High School Reform 138
Recognizing the Realities of Reform 140
Conclusion 149

References 151
Index 163
About the Authors 173

Foreword

Comprehensive Reform for Urban High Schools: A Talent Development Approach is timely and hopeful. Most urban high schools across America are in crisis, one that our political and education leaders are just now beginning to confront. This book provides a promising, research-based design to help address the seemingly intractable problems of large, comprehensive urban high schools. It shows that significant improvement in student achievement and in promotion and graduation rates is possible, even in the lowest performing urban high schools.

In most urban high schools, large numbers of students enter 9th grade with poor preparation and extremely low skills in reading and math. Many young people are deeply alienated from schools, and disconnected from adults in the broader society. As young people move through the high school years, students drop out in alarming numbers. Postsecondary enrollment rates are extremely low, and, of those relatively few who do enter 2- or 4-year institutions, growing numbers must take one or more remedial courses when they get to college, and face reduced odds of earning a degree. In short, at a time when high schools must provide a pathway to postsecondary education for all students, most urban high schools provide a pathway to nowhere.

The movement to raise standards and strengthen accountability is finally making it difficult to ignore our lowest-performing high schools. But thus far it has failed to provide much of a solution. While a handful of cities—largely with the support and encouragement of private foundations such as the Carnegie Corporation of New York and the Bill and Melinda Gates Foundation—are beginning ambitious district-wide high school reform initiatives, many urban leaders, while increasingly aware of the problem, cannot yet see the steps to a solution. Further, the bureaucratic, political, fiscal, and human resource challenges that plague urban areas make it exceedingly difficult for many state and local leaders to formulate an action plan.

As this book demonstrates, there are no quick fixes or silver bullets. Yet it also demonstrates that many of the problems in poor performing urban high schools can and will yield to the persistent application of research-based solutions.

The Talent Development Model provides a coherent and powerful design that integrates research findings about what works into practical school structures, process, and instructional strategies. It creates smaller, more-personalized learning communities, through 9th grade academies and upper-level career academies that build connections between academic and applied learning and between young people and the world outside of school. It sets high expectations and standards, providing a college preparation curriculum for all students and eliminating tracking and dead-end courses. For students who are behind, it couples rigorous academic courses with additional time and intensive instruction that is challenging and engaging and that builds on rather than ignores each student's intellectual strengths. It promotes a collaborative culture among school staff, and provides ongoing, high-quality professional development for teachers with the support of an on-site coach.

Talent Development is a solid approach, though not the only approach to transforming urban high schools. High Schools That Work, developed by the Southern Regional Education Board, has also demonstrated results, although it is just beginning to establish partnerships with large, urban, high-poverty districts. There is no shortage of ideas. The future of urban high school reform lies not in a single approach but in creating a system that provides multiple pathways and varied amounts of time for *all* young people to meet the academic standards that will open the doors to college.

If we fail to transform our urban high schools, it won't be due to a shortage of sound ideas or research-based practices, though more of both are clearly needed. Rather, the lessons from both the success and setbacks during early implementation of Talent Development in high schools in Baltimore and Philadelphia make clear the importance of mobilizing and sustaining the political will for real change. Ultimately, transforming urban high schools requires state and local policy makers, union and community leaders, parents and educators, to work together to provide the necessary resources, policies, political support, stable leadership, and time. In this regard, perhaps the most important contribution that *Comprehensive Reform for Urban High Schools: A Talent Development Approach* makes is it takes away the excuses for failing to act.

Michael Cohen
The Aspen Institute
Former Assistant Secretary of Education
December 2001

Acknowledgments

At its core, high school reform is a collective enterprise. Reform efforts in each of the schools we describe in this book would have been impossible without the courage, drive, dedication, and hard work of a great number of people. We especially acknowledge the leadership team, faculty, and staff at Patterson High School, whose pioneering efforts in 1994–97 transformed a failing high school into a place of learning and hope for its students. Their work paved the way for other troubled high schools, and has helped restore public faith in urban youth and the schools they attend. This book is dedicated to them, and to all of the teachers, administrators, students, and parents who have worked with us over the past six years to make their schools more engaging and effective.

This book also would not have been possible without the intellectual and practical contributions of many of our colleagues at the Center for Research on the Education of Students Placed At Risk (CRESPAR). We are indebted to A. Wade Boykin for his inspiring vision of a Talent Development approach to education that holds all students "at-promise" rather than at-risk. Robert Slavin, Nancy Madden, Doug Mac Iver, and Joyce Epstein have provided invaluable examples as they have developed, implemented, and scaled up their own reform programs. Velma LaPoint, Sam Stringfield, Barbara Wasik, Robert Cooper, Amanda Datnow, Martha Mac Iver, Steve Plank, Alta Shaw, Leslie Jones, and Maria Waltemeyer have all served as sounding boards or have directly contributed curricular and organizational components to the Talent Development High School (TDHS) reform model. We are also grateful to Barbara Colton, Gerry Hicks, and all of the Talent Development facilitators and staff who have made the program and this book possible.

Over the past 6 years, we have had the pleasure of working with individuals outside of CRESPAR who share our passion for high school reform and have dedicated their professional lives to improving education for urban youth. We thank Bill Morrison for applying his vision, commitment, and considerable talents to growing TDHS beyond Patterson; scale-up would have been unimaginable without his leadership. We also are indebted to Bonnie Erickson, Mildred Harris, and Charles Highsmith, three strong high school principals who took great risks and achieved great things in their schools, and who continue to make important contributions to Talent Development and urban education. We also thank our colleagues at the Philadelphia Education Fund—Nancy McGinley, Rochelle Nichols Solomon, and Betsey Useem—for their partnership and skilled guidance of TDHS in Philadelphia, and University of Pennsylvania sociologist Ruth Neild for her rigorous research contributions.

This book would have been impossible without the support of forward-thinking policymakers. We thank the U.S. Department of Education's Office of Educational Research and Improvement (OERI) and Office of Vocational and Adult Education (OVAE) for the innovative grant programs that support our work. We especially acknowledge the leadership of Michael Cohen, Patricia McNeil, Kent McGuire, and the tremendous support and guidance of Susan Talley, George Spicely, Ok Park, and Ollie Moles.

Teachers College Press editors, specifically series editors Gary Natriello and Aaron Pallas, and development editor Susan Liddicoat, provided invaluable guidance and substantive suggestions that improved our manuscript immeasurably as we moved from draft to final copy. Their sustained support and persistent but ever positive prodding has been much appreciated.

Finally, this book would be incomplete without honoring our spouses, friends, and families whose love, faith, inspiration, and support kept us all going as we struggled to simultaneously build a program and write about it. We hope this effort to put our knowledge and experiences down on paper will make them proud, as well as make a positive contribution to society and future

Comprehensive Reform for Urban High Schools

A Talent Development Approach

PART I

What Must (and Can) Be Done: Restructuring Urban High Schools

CHAPTER 1

Introduction: The Challenge

It is time for a reformulation of the purposes and means of secondary education for youth of senior high school age in the twenty-first century.
—Jurgen Herbst, *The Once and Future School: Three Hundred and Fifty Years of American Secondary Education,* p. 208

It's time for someone to put their foot down, someone who cares.
—Patterson High School student

During a recent visit to an inner-city high school, the frustration level was palpable. For years, staff had struggled to get a majority of their students to pass the state's most basic functional exams required for graduation. Their failure had prompted the state to threaten reconstitution, or takeover, if the school did not make rapid improvements in its scores, as well as in its overall climate, attendance, and promotion rates. At the same time, the state was phasing in new high school tests designed to assess not only basic skills, but high-level mastery of advanced material in all core academic subjects. How was the school going to prepare for success on these new tests when so many students had trouble passing the low-level, functional exams? How could teachers and administrators even focus on boosting achievement when they couldn't get half of their ninth graders off the streets, out of the halls, and into class on a regular basis? What options and alternatives were available to them?

Over the past decade, state and district authorities have created needed pressure for educational reform by raising standards and emphasizing accountability. This pressure, however, has been accompanied by little concrete guidance or sustained support. The fact is that many urban high schools are institutions in crisis, and without viable alternatives, they will remain so. No amount of pressure, threats, new tests, or even ritualized, annual professional development conferences are going to effect substantial change in our most troubled urban high schools. Schools will continue to flounder, and the potential of too many urban youths will remain unrealized, until we take the bold steps of crafting, communicating, and implementing new approaches to high schooling that work for urban students.

To date, high school reform in urban areas has primarily consisted of targeted programs that serve relatively few students. These include small college preparatory or career-focused programs within a comprehensive high school, or entirely separate magnet high schools with selective entrance criteria that draw the most academically motivated students from across the city. On the other end of the reform spectrum, urban districts have established alternative education programs for students with serious behavior problems or histories of criminal involvement. Some urban districts also are supporting charter schools—small, independent programs that represent a wide variety of experimental curricula and teaching techniques.

None of these targeted reforms address the needs of the majority of urban students who continue to attend large, nonselective neighborhood high schools. Anyone familiar with these schools knows that the needs of the students who attend them are great. In a recent study, Neild and Balfanz (2001) analyzed the distribution of risk factors among ninth graders attending the 22 public, nonselective high schools in Philadelphia. In 17 of these 22 high schools, *fewer than 20%* of the enrolled freshman were what might be considered "typical" ninth graders—on-age, not enrolled in special education, and whose math and reading abilities exceeded a seventh-grade level. In the five remaining schools, the proportion of ninth graders who did not possess any of these risk factors ranged from just over one-fifth to less than one-half. These and other data we cite later in this chapter suggest that the majority of students entering public, nonselective, urban comprehensive high schools are at risk of failure and eventually dropping out.

Data further show that most of these high schools, which are typically characterized by chronic low attendance, high mobility, and low achievement, have not succeeded in reducing the risk for their students. For example, in a typical comprehensive high school in Baltimore in 1996–97, three-quarters of the students had missed more than a month of school by the end of the school year. Only two-thirds of the school's ninth graders attended on any given day. Only one-third of the ninth graders had passed a seventh-grade-level functional math test required by the state. It is not surprising that these schools face high-stakes testing with a large measure of anxiety.

One of the most dramatic measures of dysfunction in Baltimore's comprehensive high schools is the sharp decline in grade-level enrollment as students progress from the 9th to the 12th grade. In 1993–94, the city's nine zoned comprehensive high schools enrolled 6,405 9th graders. In 1996–97, the 12th graders in these nine schools totaled only 1,689, representing little more than one-quarter of the freshmen 4 years earlier. In contrast, the 12th graders in Baltimore's selective magnet high schools in 1996–97 represent over three-quarters of the freshman class 4 years earlier. Even the city's vocational and alternative high schools surpassed the large, zoned high schools on this measure, with ratios of 12th to 9th graders over this time period equaling 59% and 68%, respectively.

Moreover, comparing enrollment trends in each of these types of schools shows that the outflow of students from the nine neighborhood high schools is not the result of students transferring from these schools to stronger schools within the district or into alternative schools better suited to their needs. All high schools in Baltimore have fewer tenth graders than ninth graders enrolled, and the pattern holds across the 4 years of high school. When the entire Baltimore City high school class of 1997 graduated, it had 61% fewer members than were enrolled in the ninth grade in 1993 (Maryland State Department of Education, 1997, 1999).

An analysis of this proxy dropout measure (the ratio of 12th-grade enrollment to 9th-grade enrollment 4 years earlier) in urban districts across the country shows that the Baltimore City Public School system (BCPSS) is far from atypical. A study of high schools in the central school districts of the 35 largest cities in the United States examined two cohorts, the class of 1992 and the class of 1995, to determine the percentage of freshman to reach 12th grade 4 years later, a statistic Balfanz and Legters (2001) refer to as a school's "promoting power." The study revealed that between 40 and 50% of the sampled high schools in these large cities promoted fewer than 50% of their 9th graders to the 12th grade over each 4-year period. Moreover, from the 1989–92 cohort to the 1992–95 cohort, there was an increase in the number of schools that promoted fewer than 50% of their 9th graders to 12th grade, and a significant increase in the number of schools with extremely weak promoting power—where the senior class was at least 70% smaller than the freshman class 4 years earlier.

It could be argued that the large number of 9th graders compared to 12th graders in urban comprehensive high schools is due to the large number of students who repeat the 9th grade and who hence might go on to graduate in large numbers, only later than their cohort mates. Recent analysis of 9th-grade repeaters in Chicago and Philadelphia, however, does not support this notion (Neild & Balfanz, 2001; Roderick, Choing, & DeCosta, 1998). In an ongoing study of Philadelphia high schools, for example, only 9% of the students who repeated 9th grade got back on track and graduated on time, and only another 21% are still in school. The overwhelming majority (70%) of the students who were retained in 9th grade have dropped out, gone to jail, been expelled, or left the district to an unknown destination (Neild, 2000).

National and local data clearly show that too many urban high schools are failing to educate, promote, and graduate the majority of the students who attend them. The obvious question is what can be done? In the early 1980s, the seminal report *A Nation at Risk* opened the door for an important wave of critique of American public secondary education. Actual reforms, however, have been implemented primarily at the elementary and middle school levels, with many arguing that high school was "too late" to help struggling students. Hence, while critiques of secondary school organization and pedagogy abound, practical alternatives remain undeveloped.

This book is about solutions to the challenge of improving urban high schools. As a team of researchers and developers based at Johns Hopkins University, we have worked for more than half a decade with several large, urban, nonselective high schools to develop and implement a whole-school reform model that holds promise for improving learning environments and providing higher quality education for all students. This approach, called the Talent Development High School (TDHS), includes organizational, curricular, and instructional strategies that, when taken together, create a comprehensive restructuring program for high schools. Talent Development embraces the current movement in educational reform away from piecemeal reform that touches only a few students toward the development of comprehensive or "whole-school" restructuring models. We also support the view that externally developed school reform designs provide promising options for school improvement (Stringfield & Datnow, 1998), but only when combined with school-based leadership, energy, and ingenuity. In 1997, the movement toward whole-school reform supported by specific reform models received substantial support and recognition through federal legislation that allocated $145 million for the implementation of comprehensive school reform across the country (P.L. 105-78). The Talent Development High School was named in this legislation as one of the few whole-school reform models designed specifically for high schools (Herman, 1999).

Grounded in the real-world experiences of restructuring high schools in Baltimore and Philadelphia, this book is intended to make education practitioners, policymakers, reformers, and researchers more aware of the elements of the Talent Development approach, its potential, and the challenges of implementation. Before delving into the details of our "solution," however, we begin by articulating the need for a new approach. This need, we argue below, is rooted in the anachronistic character of the traditional comprehensive high school and in the social, cultural, economic, and demographic changes that have had a devastating impact on urban education.

A HISTORICAL DIVIDE IN SECONDARY EDUCATION

In *The Second Industrial Divide,* Piore and Sabel (1984) argue that we are living through a crucial historical moment in which the dominance of mass production as the ideal form of industrial organization is being challenged by the demands of rapidly changing and increasingly diverse global markets. Effectively responding to these markets, in their view, means moving away from reliance on the rigid, standardized, fixed-use technology of the assembly line coordinated through a system of hierarchical control. In its place, Piore and Sabel favor a more responsive alternative that involves use of general purpose technology to make a variety of products, and skilled, knowledgeable workers capable of performing multiple and changing tasks within a flexible, decentralized management structure.

The roots of this alternative form, which Piore and Sabel call flexible specialization, can be found in the nineteenth century, craft-based collective where skilled workers learned from each other and collaborated within small production units. In their account, craft production and mass production struggled for dominance for a brief time near the end of the nineteenth century. Due to a convergence of social and geographic forces, and technological and economic choices, mass production emerged supreme. Piore and Sabel argue that now, at the beginning of the twenty-first century, social, technological, and economic changes are once again presenting us with a historical divide and, for them, the choice is clear. Flexible specialization based on an advanced craft model of production is the right path for prosperity and humanity in a rapidly changing and increasingly interconnected world.

What does this have to do with education reform? We posit that high school education in the United States also is facing a second historical divide. As in industry, the first historical divide in secondary education occurred at the turn of the twentieth century, and is embodied in the tension between the National Education Association's Committee of Ten on Secondary Studies' report published in 1893 and a second report released in 1918 by the Commission on the Reorganization of Secondary Education called the Cardinal Principles of Secondary Education. Commissioned by the National Education Association to clarify the character and purpose of American secondary education, the vision for secondary schooling presented by the Committee of Ten supported a common, college-preparatory curriculum for all students. The committee rooted its recommendations in a firm belief that students could learn in a rigorous academic program, regardless of class background (Herbst, 1996; Tyack, 1974; Tyack & Hansot, 1982; Wraga, 1994).

Twenty-five years later, the Cardinal Principles report emerged in response to increasing demands for vocational and "life skill" education rooted in the common perception that many students would not benefit from college preparatory education since most would not be going on to college. The spirit behind the Cardinal Principles was to create high schools that would model and reproduce democratic ideals through a comprehensive curriculum that would both respond to the diverse (academic, vocational, and social) needs of each student *and* unify students in a common culture. Lurking between the lines, however, were racist and classist assumptions held by many at the time that the masses of students entering high school, especially recently arrived immigrant children, were not capable of advanced academic work.

The large, comprehensive high school with specialized curricular tracks and bureaucratic organizational structure school envisioned in the Cardinal Principles became the dominant form of secondary education for the remainder of the twentieth century. Changes and recommendations for reform made along the way, such as the addition of a general education track to the original vocational/academic structure, were largely attempts to more fully realize, rather than call into question, the Cardinal Principles ideal (e.g., Conant, 1959, 1967).

By mid-century, however, attitudes and beliefs about differential education began to shift. In the 1954 Supreme Court decision *Brown v. The Board of Education,* the civil rights movement ended legal racial segregation in public education. The rigidly and explicitly tracked nature of the comprehensive high school itself was called into question amidst the cultural, social, and political upheaval of the 1960s and 1970s. Responding to the civil rights and feminist movements, educators, parents, and activists challenged the legitimacy of differential education for students based on gender or highly suspect measures of "intelligence" that masked continued segregation of students by race and social class. In *Tracking Inequality,* Lucas (1999) identifies the beginning of this shift as an "unremarked revolution" whereby, in response to equity concerns, high schools in many urban areas dismantled official track programs during the late 1960s and 1970s. Lucas writes that "by 1981 a majority of high schools had no formal mechanism of program assignment and thus no formal means of tracking" (p. 1). His research shows, however, that students continued to be tracked in a less explicit way at the course level and that outcomes for traditionally disadvantaged students have remained poor (and may even have worsened) in spite of the supposed shift toward a more egalitarian system. In this book, we join Lucas in arguing that these findings speak to the need for a new form of high schooling that genuinely provides all students with the information and support they need to reach their highest potential.

Other research has led many to criticize the effectiveness of the comprehensive high school and its failure to effectively respond to rapidly changing social and economic conditions. A series of studies and national reports released in the 1980s identified many shortcomings to the organization, curriculum, and instructional practices found in traditional comprehensive public high schools (Boyer, 1983; Carnegie Forum on Education and the Economy, 1986; Goodlad, 1984; Oakes, 1985; Powell, Farrar, & Cohen, 1985; Sizer, 1984).

In general, researchers have found what practitioners have known for many years—that many students (as well as teachers and administrators) feel apathetic and alienated from school; that the curriculum is fragmented, superficial, and increasingly disconnected from the changing world beyond school; and that high schools offer students highly differentiated and unequal learning opportunities. One study compared high schools with shopping malls that offer quality service and products only to those students with the resources to demand them while allowing the majority of students to pass through an unfocused, watered-down curriculum with very little effort (Powell, Farrar, & Cohen, 1985). Even well-funded, elite public high schools have been found to offer vastly unequal learning opportunities to different groups of students (Matthews, 1998).

Until about 1970, young people who had dropped out of high school or who had graduated without the coursework needed to attend college could find living wage employment in the robust manufacturing sector. Since then, the proportion of employment in the manufacturing sector has dropped by 50%, from nearly a third of all jobs in 1970 to under 15% in 2000, with continued declines projected through 2006. A rapidly expanding service sector now represents the largest number of employment opportunities. Many of the low-skilled jobs in the service sector are extremely low paid, however, with higher-paying jobs reserved for those with higher skills and educational levels. Of the 25 occupations with above-average pay and the largest employment growth projected for 1996–2006, 18 require at least a bachelor's degree, and are concentrated in computer technology, health care, and education services. Occupations that require a bachelor's degree are projected to grow the fastest, nearly twice as fast as the average for all occupations. While some occupations with above-average earnings do not require a college degree (e.g., some health care positions, automotive mechanics), most of these require some postsecondary training, especially as these fields become increasingly reliant on computer-based technology (U.S. Bureau of Labor Statistics, 2001).

Structured to provide a college-bound education for only a few students, comprehensive high schools run counter to democratic ideals, and leave too many students woefully unprepared for increasingly global and technological workplaces that are demanding high-level skills and some form of postsecondary education. With its tracked structure and highly differentiated learning opportunities, the traditionally organized comprehensive high school has become an anachronism, no longer preparing students for the world that has changed around them. It is not surprising that the end of the 1990s has seen groups of activists, philanthropists, scholars, and policymakers engaged in serious debate about the past, present, and future of the American comprehensive high school (Hammack, 2000).

THE URBAN CHALLENGE

The outdated character of comprehensive public high schools is magnified in urban districts. Unlike their suburban counterparts, urban schools face the additional challenge of economic and demographic changes that have brought an unprecedented concentration of poor, minority, and linguistically and ethnically diverse students to their doors—students who have always had more difficulty succeeding in traditional high schools. Since 1940, suburban development has prompted an ongoing outflow of middle-class residents from urban centers, a trend that has been exacerbated in recent decades by the closing of manufacturing plants. From 1940 to 1980, the proportion of residents living in central cities within a standard metropolitan statistical area (SMSA) dropped more than 22% (Rusk, 1996). By 2000, the central cities of once thriving metropolises such as Chicago, Philadelphia, Cleveland, Detroit, St. Louis, and Baltimore had experienced severe population losses, with declines ranging from 20% to nearly 60% (U.S. Census Bureau, 2000). These numbers would be even greater if some of this population loss had not been offset by the largest wave of immigration since the turn of the century. The number of foreign-born residents living in the United States has nearly tripled since 1970, with the majority settling in urban areas (Center for Immigration Studies, 1998). Though there is debate on the ultimate impact of immigration on our economy (many argue that it is a positive force), the immediate impact on schools is a challenge to educate students from increasingly diverse cultural and linguistic backgrounds.

A major consequence of this shift in population has been an increased concentration of poverty in inner cities, especially among African American and other minority groups. In spite of a declining population, poverty rates in Baltimore, for example, rose from 18% in 1970 to 24% in 1997, while the much lower rates in the growing counties around Baltimore declined during this period. By 1990, almost all poor neighborhoods (92 of 103) in the region were located in Baltimore, and almost half of the city's neighborhoods were poor (Rusk, 1996). In 1997, 32.4 or nearly a full third of all school-age children lived below the poverty line, compared with 13.5% across the state and 18.4% nationwide (U.S. Census Bureau, 2000).

Though regional variation exists, many cities have experienced similar trends. Poverty rates nearly doubled in many large cities since the early

1980s, making urban students more than twice as likely to attend high-poverty schools (schools in which more than half the students qualify for free or reduced-price lunch) than their nonurban counterparts. Not only poor, but minority students are overrepresented in urban schools; while urban school districts enroll only one-quarter of public schoolchildren in the United States, over one-third of the nation's poor students and nearly half its minority students attend school in urban areas ("Quality Counts '98," 1998).

Caught between an increase in poverty rates and an eroding tax base, urban centers struggle with fewer resources to serve a needier population. In contrast to Powell, Farrar, and Cohen's (1985) shopping malls, Louis and Miles (1990) compare urban high schools to inner-city mini-marts, "run-down and overpriced" offering "a limited selection of shoddy goods for their customers" (p. 3). The particular challenges urban high schools face are many and include the following:

Fewer Resources

Central city schools not only serve an educationally needier population of students; they also face the challenges of aging facilities that often require expensive maintenance and renovation, competition with wealthier districts for teachers, and a tax base that has dwindled in recent decades as residents have moved out of the city. These conditions arguably make urban education costlier than in other more advantaged settings. Yet, in an analysis of 1993–94 U.S. Census data, urban districts spent $500 less per pupil than their suburban counterparts ("Quality Counts '98," 1998). A different data set from 1996–97 (the most recent year for which data is available) shows suburban and central city per pupil expenditures to be virtually identical, and expenditures in districts serving 15% or more students in poverty remain from $200 to $500 less per student than in wealthier districts (U.S. Department of Education, 2000). While these gaps may not seem large on the surface, they are substantial when the needs of urban schools and students are taken into account.

Poor Prior Preparation

National data show stark achievement gaps among pre-high school students in math, science, and reading, with far more urban students scoring below basic levels than their nonurban counterparts ("Quality Counts '98," 1998). This means that most students are entering urban high schools with extremely poor prior preparation. In Baltimore, for example, in the 1999–2000 school year, 60% of ninth graders passed the basic Maryland functional test in math and 76% passed the functional writing test, compared with statewide averages of 85% and 92%, respectively. The picture is bleaker in the city's eight large, nonselective neighborhood high schools that draw from a specified attendance zone, in contrast to the citywide selective magnet high schools. In the eight zoned schools, less than half (47%) of ninth graders passed the math test and two-thirds (67%) passed the writing test (Maryland State Department of Education, 2001). These basic skills tests, however, are of a fairly low level and do not reflect the fact that nearly three-quarters of Baltimore's ninth graders are several years below grade level in reading and math (Legters & Durham, in press).

School Climate

The high concentration of poverty among students in the schools and in surrounding neighborhoods also means that issues of health, safety, and early transitions into adult roles loom larger in the daily operation of urban high schools. Nearly half of the teachers in urban districts characterize physical conflicts among students as moderate or serious problems, compared with less than a third in nonurban districts ("Quality Counts '98," 1998).

Diversity and Segregation

Urban high schools face higher levels of academic, linguistic, and cultural diversity than nonurban high schools. Since 1970, the proportion of all students who are children of immigrants tripled from 6.3% to reach nearly 20% by 1997, with nearly half living in poverty (Ruiz-de-Velasco & Fix, 2000). Fewer than half of secondary school students with limited English proficiency, however, receive LEP instruction. Diversity among urban learners also results from the larger numbers of students who require special or individualized services. The typical nonselective high school in Baltimore, for example, must provide special education services to 20% of its students, compared with 12% statewide and less than 1% in the city's magnet high schools (Baltimore City Public School System, 1997).

The diversity urban high schools face, however, is diversity within majority minority student populations. The predominance of students of color in urban high schools (in some cases reaching over 90%) has led scholars to argue that increasing racial segregation has completely supplanted the democratizing ideal of the comprehensive high school (Orfield & Eaton, 1996; Rivkin, 1994; Rury, 1999). Such segregation not only accompanies increased concentrations of low-income and impoverished students in urban schools, creating greater need. It also contributes to the cultural and linguistic isolation experienced by many minority urban residents. Such segregation and isolation likely weakens the political base for urban policymakers seeking education resources from majority White state legislatures and citizenry who have little experience of poverty or do not identify with the importance of educating minority youth.

Politics

Finally, many urban city school systems are very large and mired down in bureaucratic inertia, complicated politics, and short-term leadership, leaving high schools both unsupported and subject to constantly shifting priorities (Louis & Miles, 1990; "Quality Counts '98," 1998). The average urban superintendent serves fewer than 3 years. In the majority (51) of urban districts, superintendents have served between 1 and 5 years, and nearly a third are led by superintendents who have served for 1 year or less ("Quality Counts '98," 1998). In his book *Spinning Wheels: The Politics of Urban School Reform,* Hess (1999) argues that the revolving door of leadership in urban systems results in what he terms "policy churn." New superintendents feel compelled to introduce new reforms to show their constituents that they are effective and can make a difference. Improvements in chronically troubled urban school systems rarely occur in such a short time period, however, and constant policy changes brought on by frequent leadership changes do little more than serve that leader's image. In fact, continually unfulfilled expectations for improvement leave teachers disillusioned and resistant to further change.

Given these challenges, it is not surprising that urban high schools fare worse than their nonurban counterparts on most measures, including achievement, dropout, and graduation rates. Only from one-third to less than one-half of students in urban districts score at the basic level or higher in reading, mathematics, and science, compared with over two-thirds of students in nonurban districts. High schools in urban districts, on average, lose over half of their students between freshman and senior year, compared to a nationwide average of less than a third. At just under 10%, the single-year dropout rate for urban districts is nearly twice the national average; some urban districts struggle with annual dropout rates as high as 20% ("Quality Counts '98," 1998). Cohort analyses studying the same group of students over 4 years of high school suggest that urban dropout rates in some schools may exceed 50% (Mac Iver, Legters, & Durham, in press). These conditions are disastrous for young adults who will need post-high school education credentials to find living wage employment in an economy where low-skill jobs are becoming increasingly scarce (Singh, in Kretovics & Nussel, 1994).

PURPOSE AND PLAN OF THE BOOK

Clearly there is much need for change in urban, public comprehensive high schools. To date, however, the reform landscape in public education has been dominated by research and practical initiatives aimed toward elementary and middle-level education. The few reform efforts aimed at high schools have been either piecemeal—focusing on just one subgroup of students—or have relied on broad principles, processes, and networks rather than facilitated implementation of specific organizational and instructional strategies. Those that do promote specific strategies tend to emphasize just one strategy, small learning communities or block scheduling, for example, and do not offer an adequate framework for comprehensive improvement. The upshot is that high schools, especially urban high schools serving large numbers of at-risk students, have been left with little concrete guidance and support for whole-school reform.

Breaking Ranks, the report of the National Association of Secondary School Principals (1996), and the New American High Schools Initiative (which includes a New Urban High Schools component) of the U.S. Department of Education, have begun to identify specific strategies for high school reform. To date, however, *Breaking Ranks* and New American High Schools offer only snapshots of a handful of exemplary high schools using these various strategies. The purpose of this book is to offer an in-depth discussion of the different reforms, how they can fit together in a real-world model of whole-school change, and the benefits and challenges of implementing them in troubled urban high schools.

The next chapter presents the Talent Development response to the challenge of urban high school reform. We discuss the drawbacks of high school reform approaches to date, and argue for a whole-school, strategy-based approach. We then present the educational philosophy behind the Talent Development approach to restructuring urban high schools. At core, this philosophy states that *all* students have gifts and talents, and that schools can help *all* students develop high-level skills by providing adequate support and learning opportunities. To do this, high schools must implement far-reaching, comprehensive reforms that go beyond the usual piecemeal recommendations for change. This chapter then details each of the essential organizational, curricular, and instructional components of the Talent

Development High School model, and discusses how these components can be phased in to achieve comprehensive restructuring.

In Part II, we present a detailed case study of whole-school high school restructuring using the Talent Development approach based on our experience in Baltimore. Chapter 3 describes the context of high school reform in Baltimore. The discussion addresses state-level school reconstitution efforts, state-district tensions expressed through education equity and funding lawsuits, and leadership instability at the district level. We then turn to the school level, focusing on the history and conditions of Baltimore high schools in general and Patterson High School in particular. The remainder of Chapter 3 describes the partnership between Patterson and the Johns Hopkins Center for Research on the Education of Students Placed At Risk (CRESPAR) and Patterson's initial process of planning for whole-school reform.

Chapter 4 shows how the reforms implemented at Patterson affected school climate, staff collaboration, student attendance, promotion, dropout rates, and achievement. Data are drawn from climate surveys, focused interviews, and participant observation at school sites as well as from district data. Evidence from Patterson High School is compared to control schools and averages across other nonselective neighborhood high schools in Baltimore.

In Part III, we set forth some of the challenges to creating Talent Development High Schools (TDHS). Chapters 5 and 6 lay out the lessons we have learned about the human and technical challenges to restructuring large, urban comprehensive highs school using the Talent Development approach. We examine (1) elements of an effective planning process and rethinking of how resources and power are distributed and used within the school; (2) the challenge of maintaining whole-school cohesion in a multiple-academy organizational structure; (3) naming and negotiating school and district politics and policies that can undermine reform efforts; and (4) anticipating and addressing difficult technical issues such as staffing and scheduling a multiacademy school with extended periods and interdisciplinary teams. Our lessons learned are grounded in examples from early planning and implementation efforts in Baltimore and Philadelphia high schools.

In Chapter 7, we show how we have applied the lessons presented in Chapters 5 and 6 to improve and more successfully replicate the Talent Development model. This chapter draws on rich qualitative and quantitative data from third-party sources to show how the model has helped turn around two troubled high schools in Philadelphia—Strawberry Mansion and Edison High Schools. It also shows positive results from field testing and implementing the TDHS ninth-grade instructional improvement program in Baltimore and Philadelphia. Designed to provide materials and professional development to enable teachers to help the many students who enter high school with poor prior preparation, this program taught us important lessons about how to overcome the notorious difficulties of instructional improvement. We share these lessons in this chapter.

The conclusion, Chapter 8, summarizes the major points of the book, discusses the need to achieve a balance between "blueprint" and "involvement/empowerment" approaches to whole-school restructuring, points to other high schools and districts that are adopting reform approaches strikingly similar to those woven together in the Talent Development model, and looks forward with a call for a national urban high school restructuring movement.

This book reflects our work at the nexus of research, policy, and practice, and hence should appeal to anyone with an interest in improving urban high schools. One of our primary goals is to give school- and district-based education practitioners a blueprint for whole-school reform at the high school level that can be adapted and used as a concrete guide for their own reform efforts. By describing how a set of interrelated, research-based strategies can be woven together and implemented in real urban high schools, this book will provide practitioners with knowledge of an alternative to traditional high school organization and practice. We hope to engage administrators and teachers, as well as policymakers, in discussions about how public secondary education can be restructured to provide a high-quality education for all students, especially in large urban high schools.

CHAPTER 2

The Talent Development Response

As pointed out in the previous chapter, public comprehensive high schools have been criticized as places where unchallenging curriculum, uninspired instruction, and unequal learning opportunities produce chronic apathy, poor achievement, and high dropout rates. Throughout the late 1980s and the 1990s, such criticisms stimulated the development and implementation of a growing number of reform efforts in high schools across the country. Unfortunately, these reforms touched only a small number of students and, in most cases, followed the same logic of division and tracking that underlies traditional high school organization. Similar to the separation of students into academic, general, or vocational tracks, such reforms as pull-out compensatory education, special education, magnet programs, dropout prevention programs, single-career academies, or other types of school-within-a-school programs all single out some students to receive special services while leaving intact the basic organizational and instructional features of the large, comprehensive high school.

In many large, urban school districts, piecemeal and selective programs have recently come under fire for exacerbating educational inequity by "creaming off" the most academically motivated students and most talented teachers (Jeter, 1998). In some cities, the tracking impulse behind these approaches has created a two-tiered system in which qualified students attend citywide magnet schools, leaving the nonselective neighborhood high schools with fewer resources to educate needier students. Such strategies virtually condemn the majority of urban high school students to an underclass education, leaving them ill prepared for the future and perpetuating the chronic poverty that plagues our nation's inner cities.

In spite of these drawbacks, experimentation in urban high schools has played a crucial role in laying the groundwork for more ambitious ventures. Spurred on by new state standards and legislative changes that allow Title I funds to be used for schoolwide reform, more failing high schools are beginning to explore *whole-school* restructuring with an eye to providing *all* students with opportunities to learn relevant, high-level curriculum in a safe climate of caring and support. These efforts have both stimulated and been supported by a renewed national focus on restructuring high schools as evidenced in the report *Breaking Ranks,* which calls for comprehensive changes in curriculum, instruction, assessment, school organization, professional development, community partnerships, and leadership in American high schools (National Association of Secondary School Principals, 1996). *Breaking Ranks* promotes a vision of high schools that are broken down into smaller units, emphasizes a common curriculum and interdisciplinary instruction, embraces diversity as a strength, integrates technology into all aspects of learning, and provides teachers and administrators with the time, resources, and support they need to continuously improve their school.

How can schools operationalize the vision set forth in *Breaking Ranks?* How can they move beyond piecemeal experimentation to build more effective high schools that work for all students? This chapter begins with a discussion of the problematic features of traditional high school practice and a research-based review of the various reform responses. We then show how the Talent Development approach combines multiple reform components to create the possibility of whole-school change that can improve learning opportunities for all students, not just a select few.

PROBLEMS AND CORRESPONDING SOLUTIONS

Research has traced the malaise of high schooling to several specific features of high schools, including large size, rigid curricular tracking, departmentalization, disjointed curriculum that lacks relevance, lockstep scheduling, and unsupported transitions into and out of high school.

Large Size

The large size of most public high schools was once viewed as an advantage since a large, comprehensive high school had more resources, could offer more varied courses, and served as a focal point of pride and social activity in a community (Conant, 1959). More recently, however, a growing body of evidence points out the deleterious effects of large schools on a host of student outcomes, including achievement, attendance, involvement in school activities, and dropout rates (Fowler, 1992; Lee & Smith, 2001; Oxley, 1994). These effects typically are attributed to the difficulty that students and adults have in getting to know one another well in large schools. Impersonal relationships breed a sense of anonymity, making it easier for students to act out and more difficult for adults to curb adolescent tendencies to defy adult directives. Providing services and enforcing rules in a fair and consistent manner to hundreds of students each day overwhelms the patience and talents of even the most committed teachers, administrators, and counselors. Students who feel that no one cares about them or their performance in school are more likely to act out or become disengaged and drop out of school (Fine, 1991; Klonsky, 1995; Natriello, 1987). Problems attributed to large size affect urban students more than their suburban and rural counterparts, since nearly all urban high school students attend large high schools. In 1995, 85% of high school students in urban districts attended schools that enrolled 900 or more students, compared with the U.S. average of 68% ("Quality Counts '98," 1998).

Personalized relationships are likely to be even more important in schools serving large numbers of poor and minority students, since a greater proportion of students who attend such schools require more adult attention and special services. Moreover, as young adolescents developing an awareness of their own social identities, poor and minority students also may need personal attachments to overcome a sense of alienation from what they may view as an institution designed to serve middle class Whites (Fordham & Ogbu, 1986).

Research on school size has spawned a widespread movement toward smaller schools and the creation of self-contained "houses," "charters," or small learning communities (SLCs) within large high schools. Inspired by the widely publicized success of Central Park East in New York City and strongly influenced by Sizer's Coalition for Essential Schools, SLCs have spread to high schools in Boston, Rochester, Columbus, Philadelphia, Chicago, Baltimore, parts of California, and other areas. In general, SLCs have been found to have positive effects on students' relationships with peers, teachers and staff, extracurricular participation, and a sense of community and teamwork among staff. Students participating in SLCs also have been found to have better attendance, course passage rates, and fewer suspensions compared to demographically similar students in more traditional high school settings. These same studies show, however, that the major change in organizational structure combined with local politics, lack of leadership, and scarce resources make it difficult to achieve strong implementation of SLCs on a districtwide scale. These studies further show that weak implementation limits positive outcomes for students and staff (Fine, 1994; Oxley, 1990; see also Wraga, 1999, for review).

Curricular Tracking

High schools have traditionally been organized into separate curricular tracks—college prep, general, and vocational. As pointed out in Chapter 1, this form of explicit program-level tracking had been abandoned by many high schools by the early 1980s, but tracking at the course level persists

(Lucas, 1999). The practices of tracking and curriculum differentiation have been widely criticized for creating unequal learning opportunities for high school students and reinforcing social and economic stratification in society at large (Oakes, 1985; Yonezawa, 2000). Studies show that most high school students are tracked, that students in the lower-track classes are disproportionately minority, and that general track students experience a less demanding, watered-down curriculum and much less stimulating instruction than their high-track counterparts (Braddock, 1990; Goodlad, 1984; Oakes & Lipton, 1990).

Tracking is especially problematic in urban schools where a larger proportion of students perform below grade level and fall below the national average on basic reading, math, and science tests. Most of these students are relegated to low-level courses where they have little opportunity to learn higher-order skills or take the courses they need to get into college. Lee and Eckstrom (1987) found that students in general and vocational tracks are less likely to have access to a guidance counselor to help with course selection and post-high school planning. High dropout rates and poor attendance may also be attributed to tracking, since students in general education courses are often bored, know that they are not college-bound, and see little reason to achieve in school. A study using national data found that sophomores enrolled in general and vocational tracks are three to four times more likely to drop out than students in academic programs (Barro & Kolstad, 1987).

A central feature of restructuring urban high schools is detracking instruction in favor of a common core curriculum in which all students take the same set of college preparatory courses (Lee & Smith, 1995; Newmann & Wehlage, 1995). Following recommendations of the National Commission on Excellence in Education, a core curriculum typically consists of 4 years of English; 3 or more years each of mathematics, social studies, and science; and a half-year of computer science. According to the National Center for Education Statistics, the percentage of public school districts that meet or exceed these recommendations increased from 12 to 20% between the 1987–88 and 1993–94 school years (U.S. Department of Education, National Center for Educational Statistics, 2000).

In its most rigorous form, a common core curriculum demands that all students be taught the same high-level material in each of these academic subject areas. Because many students enter high school with poor prior preparation, however, schools must put in place support systems for students to succeed in core courses. Transition courses to boost reading and math skills, flexible opportunities to learn (e.g., after-school, Saturday, and summer school programs), frequent report-card counseling, attendance incentives (since much failure is linked directly to poor attendance), and other extra-help strategies are needed to promote student success in a common core curriculum. Professional development also is required to better equip teachers with the skills and strategies to teach heterogeneous groups of students. We discuss some of these strategies in more detail in the course of this book.

The strongest arguments in favor of a common core curriculum in urban schools are found in research on Catholic and private schools. These studies show that students not only achieve more in schools that expect all students to succeed in the same set of core academic courses, but that achievement is distributed more equitably across socioeconomic class within those schools as well (Bryk, Lee, & Holland, 1993; Coleman, Hoffer, & Kilgore, 1982). Other studies that examine learning opportunities and course-taking in high schools support these findings (Council of the Great City Schools, 1998; Lee, Smith, & Croninger, 1997; for review, see McPartland & Schneider, 1996).

A recent study of detracking initiatives suggests, however, that the forces of academic differentiation run deep in high schools. Powerful parents and conflicts with the stratified nature of higher education systems can pose substantial barriers to detracking efforts (Wells & Oakes, 1996).

Departmentalization

A near-universal feature of traditional secondary schooling is organization into subject-area departments. Specialization in a particular subject area enables secondary teachers to know a subject well and hence teach the higher-level instructional content required for older students. Departmentalization, however, has been criticized for producing a superficial and fragmented curriculum that fails to engage many students. Research evidence also suggests that instructional benefits of departmentalized staffing may be offset by ways in which departmentalization detracts from a school's ability to provide an environment of caring and support for its students (Bryk, Lee, & Smith, 1990; McPartland, 1990).

Departmentalization can interfere with positive teacher-student relations by putting up procedural, psychological, and logistical barriers to teachers and students knowing one another well. Because secondary teachers' professional identities are more closely bound to the standards of a particular subject area (and often strict curricular guidelines), they may be more likely to fail students who do not meet the course requirements rather than try to help students overcome their difficulties. High school teachers typically teach five to six different classes per day with little or no interaction with teachers in other subjects who may teach those students, making it very difficult for them to know any individual student and his or her capabilities well (LaPoint, Jordan, McPartland, & Penn Towns, 1996).

To preserve the benefits of subject-area specialization but eliminate its isolating and potentially alienating aspects, restructuring high schools are experimenting with interdisciplinary teacher teaming (Lee & Smith, 2001; Newmann & Wehlage, 1995). Better known as a middle-school practice, the most prevalent form of interdisciplinary teaming is a four-teacher team made up of one teacher each of math, English, science, and social studies. These teachers share responsibility for the curriculum, instruction, evaluation, and often the scheduling and discipline of a group of 100–150 students (Alexander & George, 1981; Arhar, 1992; Mac Iver & Epstein, 1991). Like small learning communities, this arrangement is designed to help personalize the learning environment by increasing knowledge and communication among teachers, students, and parents about students' successes and problems in each subject. This sharing of students is not only supposed to provide teachers, parents, and students with a more integrated view of students' progress, but also helps students feel that there is a group of concerned adults looking out for them.

Interdisciplinary teaming also can lend more coherence and depth to the traditional academic curriculum by enabling teachers to integrate lessons across subject areas and focus on thematic units. This aspect of teaming, however, requires curricular flexibility as well as training and time for teachers to plan together. Leaders of one high school teaming experiment suggest that "changing structures and relationships precedes changing curriculum" (Ashby & Ducett, 1995/96, p. 10).

Interdisciplinary teams and subject area departments are not necessarily mutually exclusive in restructuring high schools. Department affiliation may coexist with teams by design, or may be sustained de facto if the teaming structure is implemented in such a way that it fails to provide a "new and powerful basis on which to join teachers' professional activity" (Little, 1995, p. 177). In the Talent Development model we describe in more detail later in this chapter, department heads continue to work as instructional leaders and coordinators throughout the school even as the school is reorganized around interdisciplinary small learning communities.

Relevance of Schoolwork

High dropout rates, poor attendance, and poor performance among students in vocational and general tracks are indicators that many students are disengaged and care little about school. This is attributed, in part, to teacher-centered, textbook-bound, skill-and-drill instructional techniques that dominate teaching in general track classes, especially in urban comprehensive high schools serving high-poverty students (Haberman, 1996). Apathy among students also has been attributed to a lack of connection between schoolwork and the world beyond school. Since employers do not require transcripts or other evidence of school performance, it is unclear to students who do not see themselves as college-bound how doing well in school will make a difference for their futures (Bishop, 1989). Most business leaders believe that high schools do little to prepare students for the teamwork, communication, decision making, and technological and computing skills required in changing workplaces (Resnick & Wirt, 1996; Secretary's Commission on Achieving Necessary Skills [SCANS], 1991). Poor and minority students, moreover, are even more prone to apathy in a traditional high school curriculum because they are less likely to see their experience or heritage represented in curricular materials, and often lack role models and other motivational supports for academic performance.

An emerging school-to-work or school-to-career movement is one of the most prominent reform efforts aimed at making schoolwork more relevant and engaging more students in school. Inspired by European systems and supported by the 1994 School to Work Opportunities Act, many states across the country have developed technology preparation (Tech Prep), shadowing, apprenticeship, internship, and other work-based learning programs for high school-age youth (Olson, 1997; Stern et al., 1995). High schools also are experimenting with integrating academic and vocational curricula to form focused career majors, clusters, pathways, or academies (Grubb, 1995a).

Career academies present a potentially powerful manifestation of school-to-work efforts because they combine the relevance of a career focus with the personalized environment of a self-contained small learning community. Career academies have been found to have positive effects on student performance, dropout prevention, and college attendance (Stern, Raby, & Dayton, 1992). Early evidence from an evaluation of 10 career academy programs indicates that career academy students are more motivated to attend school and view schoolwork as more relevant to their futures, and that job satisfaction and sense of belonging to a strong professional community are higher among academy teachers (Kemple, 1997). Most high schools experimenting with career academies, however, have only one academy that serves a small group of students. Grubb (1995a) points to the potential for all students in a high school to participate in a career-focused program, noting the added benefit of having students actually choose their own program which increases their attachment to school. Very few high schools are implementing multiple career academies, clusters, or majors, however, and research evidence is scant.

Compared with the school-to-work movement, efforts to make schooling and schoolwork more relevant to students' cultural background and experiences are less developed, especially at the high school level. Scholars argue that minority students are more likely to excel in educational environments that are responsive to their language, history, and culture (Boykin, 1994; Hale, 1994; Hale-Benson, 1986; Ladson-Billings, 1994). Boykin and Bailey (2000) explore how cognitive performance of low-income African-American children may be enhanced in learning contexts that integrate aspects of an Afro-cultural ethos. The study focuses on three cultural themes—movement, communalism, and verve—that the researchers argue are central to African-American culture and home life. Their findings suggest that motivation and learning may be promoted for African-American children in contexts that integrate syncopated music and movement, cooperative learning, and high variation of activities. To date, however, studies of pedagogical approaches that might be more responsive to students' different cultural backgrounds focus primarily on elementary grade students, leaving open the question of what culturally relevant pedagogy might look like for students in a later developmental stage. Multicultural curricula and language experiments (e.g., English as a Second or Other Language [ESOL], Ebonics) in general have proved controversial, and there is a great need for further experimentation and research in this area.

School Schedule

A broad critique of traditional uses of time for schooling emerged in the early 1990s (National Education Commission on Time and Learning, 1994). The rigid, "factory" model of students moving from class to class six to eight times per day is another aspect of high school organization that impedes the development of close relationships between teachers and students. Periods that are 45 to 55 minutes in length also make it difficult for teachers to complete lessons, present material in a variety of ways so that more students understand, or implement innovative approaches such as project-based, technology-based, or cooperative learning strategies. Finally, the traditional high school schedule reinforces content coverage over depth of understanding, and inhibits strategic and flexible grouping of students who need extra help in a particular area.

In an effort to move away from fragmented instruction and impersonal, factorylike environments, high schools are experimenting with alternative forms of scheduling (O'Neil, 1995). Foremost among these is block scheduling, which organizes courses around four 90-minute periods per day instead of seven or eight 50–55 minute periods per day. In the 4 x 4 block scheduling plan, students take the same four classes each day and complete them in one semester. In the alternate day (A/B) plan, students take half their classes in extended periods one day, and the other half of their classes the next day, with the pattern repeating throughout the school year (Canady & Rettig, 1995).

Block scheduling is often used to support small learning communities and interdisciplinary teaming. The four-period day supports improvements in discipline by reducing the number of class passings per day. It also supports more varied and individualized instruction by providing more time in each class period and by enabling teacher teams to change the schedule from week to week or even daily to meet the particular and changing needs of their students. One very important use of flexible block scheduling is providing extra help to students with poor academic preparation in the form of transition courses, tutoring, and targeted academic counseling.

Research on block scheduling from around the country indicates that the practice is on the rise, with scholars predicting that 75% of all high schools will be using some form of block scheduling by the early naughts (Queen & Isenhour, 1998). Studies have found that block scheduling enabled students to take a broader range of courses, reduced discipline referrals, improved attendance and achievement, and enabled teachers to offer more varied learning opportunities and give students more individual attention. One survey of 24 high schools in several states found that support for extended periods among the teachers, students, and administrators surveyed rose from 33% prior to block scheduling to 80% once block scheduling had been implemented (Hottenstein, cited in Queen, 2000). Other studies have found, however, that teachers are still prone to overuse teacher-centered lecture and drill methods and must be prepared well to use the longer period effectively (see Queen, 2000, for review).

Instruction

Instruction in traditional comprehensive high schools also has come under fire for failing to engage students in the learning process (Newmann, 1992). Some of these criticisms are related to the departmentalization and scheduling practices described above. High school teachers are typically trained to be masters of a particular subject area and receive little training on how most effectively to teach their subject to a diverse group of students (Siskin & Little, 1995). Traditional teaching methods such as lecturing, worksheets, and reliance on textbooks fail to engage many students who may tune out because they do not see the material as relevant to their lives or because they do not learn well by listening and reading. Teachers also have great difficulty covering an entire lesson in 45–55 minutes, especially if they are trying to design varied activities that will enable all students to learn the material. Finally, teachers teaching seven or eight periods in a day more or less isolated from other adults are likely to be overwhelmed with work and lack problem-solving support or intellectual stimulation, conditions that lead to alienation, apathy, and burnout among teachers (Sizer, 1984).

More "constructivist" pedagogical approaches have gained favor in recent years, encouraging educators to move away from the model of teacher as dispenser and students as passive receptacles of knowledge. Instead, these approaches assume students as active participants in learning who bring knowledge, values, and experiences into the classroom with them (Resnick, 1987a). From this assumption, the teacher's role shifts to one of facilitator or coach, designing activities that enable students to engage the course content in varied and creative ways to maximize interest and learning. In this framework, specific instructional approaches come under the headings of "active," "contextual," "project-based," "interdisciplinary," and "cooperative learning." Research has shown various forms of cooperative learning and other "student-centered" practices to be beneficial for students both in the United States and in other countries, and especially for disadvantaged students (Cohen & Lotan, 1997; Newmann, 1996; Slavin, 1986, 1994; Stevenson & Stigler, 1992; U.S. Department of Education, National Center for Educational Statistics, 2000; Wiggins & McTighe, 2000). All of these approaches are more viable in schools structured to offer longer class periods, flexible scheduling opportunities, and collaboration among teachers. (See Bevevino, Snodgrass, Adams, & Dengel, 1999, for examples of lesson plans designed for extended class periods.)

Transitions

When students make the transition into high school as ninth graders, they must negotiate a new physical space, new relationships with adults and peers, and new academic demands. Most high schools are large, bureaucratic organizations characterized by more formal rules and impersonal relationships than middle or elementary schools. Research on school transitions shows that many students struggle with the transition to high school (see Roderick, 1993, for review). Among all high school students, ninth graders tend to have the lowest grade-point averages, greatest number of disciplinary problems, and highest failure rates. In her study of one school district, Roderick (1993) found that average grades declined by 18% following the move from middle to high school. She also shows that academic failure is more likely for many students during their first year of high school. Moreover, she shows that academic failure during that year has a greater impact on students' decisions to persist in school since they are in the process of determining whether they "fit" in high school (see also Neild & Balfanz, 2001).

Successfully integrating into a traditionally organized high school is likely to be more difficult for poor and minority students. These students are generally more oriented toward work life than academics, tend to be placed in less engaging, lower-track classes, and are more likely to experience conflicts between their student role and the other roles (parent, worker, translator, gang member) they play outside of school (Bryk & Thum, 1989; Eckstrom et al., 1987; Fine, 1985, 1987; Oakes, 1985). With little personal attachment or access to extra help, many ninth graders fail courses, fall further and further behind, and ultimately become disengaged and drop out.

Roderick (1993) reviews a number of programmatic approaches designed to ease students' transition into high school. These include orientation and summer transition programs such as the Summer Training and Education Program (STEP), and targeted remediation programs that introduce students to the high school environment and provide extra help with academic coursework (see also Natriello, McDill, & Pallas, 1990). Other approaches involve creating advisories or special classes for ninth graders that emphasize personal contact between students and teachers and which focus on social support, life skills, and career awareness. Some districts are experimenting with more radical approaches that involve separating ninth graders from the rest of the school for all or part of the school day through the use of interdisciplinary teams, schools-within-a-school, or altogether separate schools (Beyers, 1997; McPartland, Jordan, Legters, & Balfanz, 1997). Other strategies include alternative settings and after-school programs that do one or all of the following: provide extra help for students, enable students to continue earning credits toward graduation while working, and address legal or personal problems that make it difficult for these students to attend regular day school.

The problematic features of traditional high schools and corresponding reforms described above are summarized in Figure 2.1.

PUTTING IT TOGETHER: THE TALENT DEVELOPMENT APPROACH

As the preceding discussion suggests, comprehensive high schools are experimenting with new approaches. Very few schools, however, have applied multiple approaches toward a whole-school reform effort with the

FIGURE 2.1. **Criticisms of Comprehensive High Schools and Reform Responses**

Criticisms	Reform Responses
Large Size	Small Schools Schools-within-a-school (houses, clusters, small learning communities)
Curriculum Tracking and Unequal Learning Opportunities	Common core curriculum
Departmentalization	Interdisciplinary teaming
Lack of Relevance	School-to-work focus Career academies Multicultural curriculum
Rigid Schedule	Flexible block scheduling Longer class periods Opportunities for extra help (flex school, Saturday school, summer school)
Teacher-Centered Instruction	Active instructional techniques (cooperative learning, project-based learning, integrating technology)
Unaided Transition to High School	Orientation and summer transition programs Advisories and special classes for freshmen Ninth-grade academies Alternative and after-school settings

aim of creating improvement for all students. The Talent Development High School program and its partner schools have attempted to do just that by showing how schools can completely reorganize fundamental institutional features to achieve meaningful schoolwide reform. We begin with a brief overview of the theoretical perspectives that undergird the Talent Development approach. We then describe the components of the Talent Development High School reform model and how they address the challenges of anonymity, apathy, and diversity faced by high schools today.

Theoretical Supports for Talent Development High Schools

The term "Talent Development" is drawn from the work of A. Wade Boykin (1994) and other education theorists who expect high standards and demanding curricula for *all* students. In Boykin's research and writings, the Talent Development approach assumes that students are "at promise" rather than at risk, that all students have gifts and talents, and that given adequate resources and supportive learning environments, all but the most severely disabled students can learn and meet high standards.

In the mid-1960s, proponents of the view that "all students can learn" were set back by a large study summarized in what is now called the Coleman Report (Coleman et al., 1966). The study found that students' socioeconomic status, race/ethnicity, and family structure were stronger predictors of their achievement than were the conditions they encountered in school. Thanks to subsequent developments in organizational theory and in theories about cognition and learning, we now are attaining more nuanced understandings of effective educational processes that challenge the findings of the Coleman Report.

School Organization. Changes in thinking about effective educational organization reflect a more general shift in organizational development theory. Since the mid-1970s, longstanding critiques of bureaucratic organization have gained widespread popularity. Centralized control, hierarchical authority structures, rigid rules and roles, and the formal, impersonal modes of communication that characterize bureaucratic organizations have been called into question for fostering apathy, alienation, rigidity, and frustration among workers, managers, and customers alike. In response, organizational theories that favor more communal workplace structures and processes have been gaining favor in industry, government, and corporations as well as in education (Deming, 1986; Senge, 1990, 2000). These structures and processes include decentralized authority and decision making, shared commitment to a common mission and set of goals, cross-unit work teams, flexible time and roles, use of data to support continuous learning and improvement, and less formal and more personalized work environments that minimize status differences and promote communication.

Educational sociologists and social psychologists have identified similar features in their research on effective educational organizations. Bryk and Driscoll (1988) defined communal organization as a key aspect of Catholic and private schools that promotes success for socioeconomically disadvantaged students. Their concept of communal organization includes small school size, teacher roles that extend beyond subject-matter specialization to include mentoring and other personal interaction with students, high levels of collegiality and joint problem-solving among staff, shared beliefs about instruction, and an ethic of caring and support. Further research has shown how these features (and associated specific restructuring practices) help create a more engaging and meaningful learning environment for students, a greater sense of efficacy and collective responsibility among adults, and conditions for ongoing reflection and organizational learning (Lee, Bryk, & Smith, 1993; Lee & Smith, 2001; Leithwood, Jantzi, & Steinbach, 1998; Newmann, 1992). While scholars rightfully challenge the uncritical adoption of new organizational and management approaches from the corporate world into education (Pallas & Neumann, 1995), research to date supports the theory that more communally organized schools create more effective teaching and learning environments for disadvantaged students.

Cognition and Learning. Contemporary theory about how children learn and debates over the most effective curricula and instructional approaches have been strongly influenced by two related strands of theory and research. Gardner's (1983, 2000) groundbreaking theory of multiple intelligences argues that our narrow emphasis on logical and verbal forms of intelligence fails to acknowledge the importance of other forms of intelligence (e.g., musical, spatial, kinesthetic, inter- and intrapersonal). By gearing our education system to support only logical and verbal ways of knowing, we make success potentially more difficult for children who learn better when curricula and instruction tap into one or more of the other forms of intelligence. The implications are obvious: if students are to achieve their highest learning potential, curricula and learning activities must be changed to match the diversity and multiplicity of learning styles they bring into the classroom.

Gardner's work is extended in the constructivist perspective mentioned earlier in this chapter during the discussion of instructional reforms. Rooted in developmental psychology theory, constructivism calls on educators to recognize that students are more motivated to learn, and learn best when they are solving problems that are relevant to them, when they are actively involved in constructing their own meanings so that abstract concepts make sense to them, and when they are able to apply what they already know to the problem-solving process (National Council of Teachers of Mathematics, 1989; Resnick, 1987a). Research supporting this view also has demonstrated that types of higher-order thinking (analyzing, judging, thinking critically) are involved in all learning and, with the right pedagogical approaches, can even be developed more fully while a student is learning the basic skills of reading, writing, and mathematics (Resnick, 1987b). A constructivist perspective not only assumes that all children *can* learn but that all children *have learned and are learning* all the time. The task then for curriculum developers and teachers is to guide that learning energy through engaging, relevant, positive, and productive activities that develop students' knowledge and skills.

Applying multiple intelligence and constructivist theories to real-world educational settings is no mean feat. Methods of cooperative, project-based, interdisciplinary, contextual, and culturally relevant teaching and learning are becoming more visible and widely accepted ideas. In practice, however, they are still the exception and high school classrooms continue to be dominated by teacher-centered, textbook-driven activity.

One reason it is so difficult to change classroom practice is the limited and acontextual nature of most pre-service and in-service teacher training. Academic coursework unrelated to teachers' daily classroom context and the fragmented, one-shot workshops that make up most district-level, one-size-fits-all professional development programs do little to prepare teachers to take on extended roles and integrate constructivist methods into their teaching. In response, the mid-1990s saw calls for new methods of professional development in which teachers take an active role in their own growth, and learning opportunities are coherent, collaborative, long range, and closely linked to the immediate contexts of teaching and school improvement (National Commission on Teaching & America's Future, 1996; National Foundation for the Improvement of Education, 1996). Indeed, many of the characteristics of new forms of professional development mirror the constructivist approaches now being recommended for students (see Fullan and Hargreaves, 1992; Little, 1993; Sparks & Hirsh, 1997; Smylie, 1996). As we demonstrate further in Chapters 6 and 7, intensive, meaningful, and sustained facilitation, training, and support for teachers and administrators are critical to the implementation of reform that affects change in a school's instructional core.

THE THEORY AND RESEARCH described above offers new ways of thinking about how we might address the serious challenges of student anonymity, apathy, and diversity that have been found to impede student motivation and learning during the adolescent years (Carnegie Task Force on Education of Young Adolescents, 1989; National Association of Secondary School Principals, 1996). The Talent Development High School reform model represents a real-world effort to put theory into practice and help high schools meet those challenges head-on. We now turn to the specifics of the reform approach.

Combating Anonymity

A reason often given by students for dropping out is their dislike for how they are treated by teachers and administrators. A positive school climate, where students and adults know each other well and where adults express care and concern for students' welfare is a key motivational element in the learning process for adolescents. However, as described in the preceding section, the sheer size and bureaucratic nature of large, comprehensive secondary schools work against the development of close personal relationships.

The Talent Development approach involves school organization reforms that break down the anonymous character of traditional, departmentalized comprehensive high schools and that create more communal learning environments characterized by positive, respectful, and caring relationships between students and adults in the school. These reforms are described in detail in the following sections.

Small Learning Communities. Small learning communities are self-contained units with their own management and instructional staff located in a separate part of the school building. Unlike other small learning community approaches, however, Talent Development High Schools are organized around two particular types of small learning communities—Ninth Grade Academies and Wall-to-Wall Career Academies.

A Ninth Grade Academy (also called a Ninth Grade *Success* Academy) is specifically designed to ease students' transition into high school and promote early success and positive attachment to school. The Ninth Grade Academy operates as a self-contained school-within-a-school located in its own part of the school building, preferably with its own entrance and computer and science lab facilities. As a school-within-a-school, the Ninth Grade Academy also has its own leadership team (made up of an academy principal and an academy leader) and dedicated faculty who teach only within the academy.

Because many large comprehensive high schools have a large ninth-grade class, the Ninth Grade Academy is typically further organized into small interdisciplinary teams of four to six teachers who shared the same 150–180 students. Each team of teachers shares a common planning period where they can discuss individual student problems, meet with parents, and coordinate and integrate activities and coursework across subjects. Responsibility for finding solutions to individual student attendance, discipline, and learning problems rests with the teacher teams. Each has a team leader and uses monthly and weekly data to set goals and monitor trends in student behavior.

Numerous activities are structured for ninth-grade students to ensure good attendance and progressive achievement that set the foundation for serious student work and ensure promotion to the next grade. Students also participate in self- and career-awareness activities that provide detailed information on high school choices and college alternatives. At the midpoint of ninth grade, students select a Career Academy that they will attend for the final 3 years of high school.

Similar to the Ninth Grade Academy, Career Academies in the Talent Development approach also are self-contained small learning communities that enroll a total of 250–350 students in grades 10 through 12. Each career academy has its own faculty and building location where students take both core academic and career-related courses. This differs from some applications of career academies in which students take only their career courses in a designated part of the building. The Talent Development approach also differs from other applications of career academies by providing a career academy for *all* upper grade students. To date, most career academies exist as single programs within a school and are often selective. In contrast, a Talent Development High School is organized around multiple career academies, often referred to as wall-to-wall academies, so that every student participates in one.

With the Ninth Grade Academy and upper-level Career Academies, all students in a Talent Development High School enjoy the benefits of more personalized relationships with adults in a small learning community setting. Other beneficial aspects of career academies as a particular type of small learning community are described below when we address reforms that provide more relevance to students' school experience.

Freshman Seminar and Upper Grade Advisors. To remain engaged in high school, students need to have the information and tools that will enable them to be successful, and to have access to trusted adults who can provide them with information and sustained support. In a large school, frequent access to guidance counselors is too often limited to students with special talents or needs, leaving the majority of students to fend for themselves as they negotiate the social and academic complexities of high school. To supplement the small learning community approach, the Talent Development model offers a freshman seminar course for incoming students. This course is designed to strengthen students' study and social skills, help them deal successfully with authority and other relationships, provide information about grades and credits they need for graduation and college entrance, and encourage exploration of college and career interests to prepare them for a wise Career Academy selection. In the upper grades, students have an advisor in their Career Academy who serves as an adult advocate and problem solver for the final 3 years of high school.

Recovery Opportunities and Support Services. The reality of adolescence today, especially for children growing up in high-poverty urban areas, is that some students will have difficulties succeeding even in a radically restructured high school. One of the goals of the Talent Development High School is to keep as many students as possible connected to school and achieving academic progress by instituting flexible options for students to earn credits.

One such option is Twilight School, an after-hours program conducted in the school building for students who have serious attendance or disciplinary problems or who are coming to the school from incarceration or from suspension from another school. Some students have difficulty attending day school regularly because they must work or care for siblings, their own children, or other family members. An after-school program enables these students to continue earning credits toward graduation. Twilight School also keeps students with behavioral problems from being distracted, and distracting others, during the regular school day. Instruction offered in small classes in the basic subjects, and other services provided by guidance and support staff, also benefits students who have trouble succeeding in the larger day school. In addition to enabling students to continue earning credits regardless of their life circumstances, an important goal of Twilight School is to help students earn their way back to regular day school by developing the coping skills to be successful there. Teachers are typically drawn from the regular day school faculty and often teach Twilight courses on alternate day schedules.

Other flexible options for students who fail one or more courses are after-hours *credit school, Saturday school,* and *summer school.* While such programs often are offered by school districts, the Talent Development approach recommends that individual schools offer these programs and that they be taught by volunteer school employees so that students maintain an attachment to the school and the adults who run it.

School, Family, and Community Partnerships. Research shows that students benefit from sustained communication and collaboration between teachers, students' families, and other community organizations concerned with children and youth (Epstein, 1991). Too often, however, parental involvement in schools tapers off as their youngsters reach high school age. When parents and community leaders are active members of a small learning community or academy, they become part of the team of adults supporting students' attachment to and progress in school. To this end, the Talent Development High School model incorporates Epstein's approach to promoting school, family, and community partnerships (see Epstein, 2001). School-based teams are trained in promoting different types of involvement and are linked to a national network of schools implementing the approach.

Combating Apathy

Adolescent students become bored and attendance suffers when they are not drawn to their classwork by the prospect of interesting and fulfilling class activities or when they see no connection between learning tasks and their own interests and futures. The Talent Development Model involves organizational and instructional reforms that fight apathy by injecting meaning into the curriculum, connecting schoolwork to students' backgrounds, interests, and goals, and enlivening lessons and learning activities with interesting and challenging applications. Specific reforms are described below.

Wall-to-Wall Career Academies. The Talent Development High School offers relevance by providing a career focus that gives coherence to the curriculum. Multiple Career Academies are developed within the school so that all upper grade students participate in an academy program. As described above, an academy is a self-contained school-within-a-school with its own faculty and building location. In addition, each academy offers a core college preparatory curriculum with different course sequences of electives and out-of-school learning opportunities tied to different career themes. When fully developed, each Career Academy has an industry advisory board to help design the course sequences, to provide internships or other experiential learning activities, and to assist teachers in blending career applications in core academic courses.

Because Talent Development High Schools are organized around multiple, or "wall-to-wall" Career Academies, the academies typically reflect distinct career areas so that every student can find a "home" that matches his or her interests. For example, a school with four Career Academies might have one that focuses on arts, one on business and finance, one on health sciences, and one on transportation and engineering. Each Career Academy then develops two or three programs, called pathways, to provide instruction and work-based learning for more specific sets of occupations within the academy theme—journalism within the Arts Academy, for example, or auto engineering within the Transportation Academy.

The Career Academy curriculum is designed to keep students' options open, by preparing them for both college and careers. Those who go directly to college after graduating from high school may continue their studies in the same field as their high school Career Academy, or they may choose a different field. Career Academy graduates who go directly into full-time work will have gained the knowledge and experience to give them an advantage in the job market. They also will have taken the necessary high school courses to qualify for college admission if they decide to resume their education. Choosing a Career Academy, therefore, does not represent an irrevocable career decision.

Still, the choice of a Career Academy should be carefully matched with students' interests at the time. Before choosing, students engage in extended self-awareness activities to gain insight into their own career interests and strengths. They are also given detailed information on the offerings and opportunities of each Career Academy. The goal is to assist each student to make a carefully considered choice of a Career Academy that will give a meaningful focus to the curriculum for the last 3 years of high school. The choice process in which students participate, and the resulting match between students' interests and their program of study, is intended to increase students' motivation and commitment to school.

Interdisciplinary, Contextual, and Blended Instruction. By making Career Academies the central organizing feature of high schooling in the upper grades, the Talent Development High School approach eliminates institutional distinctions between academic, general, and vocational tracks and encourages cross-disciplinary teaching and learning. Coursework seeks to blend academic learning and career applications. Contextual learning activities can provide several different career applications for the major units of core academic subjects. Thus, students in each Career Academy have opportunities to be involved in relevant occupational applications blended into their core academic subjects.

Four-Period Day. The core set of college preparatory academic courses and electives in a Talent Development High School are scheduled in four 90-minute periods each day. With this 4 x 4 block schedule, students can complete an entire yearlong course in one 18-week term, leaving more room in the schedule for extra help (see the double-dosing strategy, below) and for career electives and work-based learning experiences in the upper grades. As pointed out earlier, the 90-minute period also provides teachers with time to use a variety of learning activities that call for students to work individually and collectively on challenging and interesting topics. These include cooperative learning, technology, project-based, and other innovative teaching techniques designed to engage a diverse range of students.

One of the potential drawbacks of the 4 x 4 schedule is that students complete a course in one semester and then may skip a semester before they have that subject again. Foreign language, media/performing arts (e.g., band, journalism, yearbook), and advanced placement classes have been particular sticking points, but concerns over core academic course sequencing have also been raised. Queen (2000) reports creative ways in which schools have addressed these issues within the block by scheduling students to take two sequenced courses in a subject during a single year, providing special second semester elective classes that enable students to deepen and extend knowledge in a given subject (including Advanced Placement [AP]), and offering after-hours and weekend review sessions prior to AP tests. Queen also believes that AP testing should be made available each semester, given the number of schools moving to the 4 x 4 block schedule across the country.

We have found that once Talent Development High Schools begin implementing the 4 x 4 block schedule, academy leaders and schedulers find a great deal of flexibility in the daily schedule to accommodate various individual and program needs. The main priorities of TDHS are that students take the majority of their academic and elective courses within their academy, that the schedule is used to provide extra help so that all students can succeed in the common core curriculum, and that the extended period be the primary scheduling time unit.

Finding Strength in Diversity

Perhaps the greatest challenge in American education is how to produce student achievement at high performance standards in the face of the wide diversity of prior preparations among the students entering high school. The Talent Development answer is not to compromise on standards. In Talent Development High Schools all students are offered a common core college preparatory curriculum that (1) is flexible regarding time and resources for meeting different student needs; (2) provides transition learning activities for some students to prepare them for advanced work; and (3) includes abundant opportunities for recovery from course failures without being retained in grade.

The Talent Development High School approach includes a Ninth Grade Instructional Program of flexible resources, transition courses, and recovery opportunities that has been piloted and implemented in several large, urban nonselective high schools. Within the two 18-week term schedules of four extended 90-minute periods each day, many ninth-grade students in these schools are being given the equivalent of double doses in English and math by taking these subjects for extended 90-minute periods throughout the year, essentially providing them with the equivalent of 2 years of instruction in 1 year.

New transition courses in reading and mathematics are offered as a first-term learning experience for students with very poor entering skills. "Strategic Reading" is a course for students who are two or more grades below expected reading level that appeals to teenagers by (1) teaching word attack and phonetic skills with rhyming and rapping exercises within word families, and (2) using high interest level and low reading level materials in cooperative learning activities to practice vocabulary and reading skills. These students then enroll in the core English course for the second term of the ninth grade, but continue to get extra instruction and practice in basic reading skills.

"Transition to Advanced Mathematics" is a first-term ninth-grade course for students with very poor mathematical preparation and negative attitudes about the value of mathematics and their own mathematical abilities. This course addresses both skills and motivation with a blend of traditional and innovative strategies drawn from the University of Chicago School Mathematics Project and recent National Science Foundation mathematics curricula to improve students' mathematical understanding and achievement. It also covers all the topics usually found in a high-level pre-algebra course. Students move onto Algebra I for the second term of the ninth grade, with some built-in opportunities for further help on basic mathematical skills.

As mentioned earlier, a Talent Development High School also provides extra time outside of the regular school year, in summer school, Saturday school and after-hours credit school, for students to make up credits in failed courses or to get the extra learning time that may be prescribed for students who passed a core course but still are far behind most other students.

Professional Development and Technical Assistance

Implementing a comprehensive set of organizational and instructional reforms that respond to the challenges of anonymity, apathy, and diversity requires that teachers and administrators change their practice in fundamental ways. Traditional professional development approaches for high school reform (i.e., initial visionary planning assistance with only periodic implementation checks, one-shot workshops with little or no follow-up, training on instructional techniques unrelated to the curriculum teachers are using) do not provide the intensive, sustained, and on-site support that schools need to implement whole-school reforms.

The Talent Development approach to professional development may be summed up in Fullan's (2001) statement, "There is no getting around the primacy of personal contact" (p. 124). A critical component of the Talent Development approach is an on-site team of trained facilitators to support the planning and implementation of reforms, and to follow up workshops for school faculty with in-class support. Ordinarily, this team consists of a half-time organizational facilitator and three half-time instructional facilitators—one in English, one in math, and one to support the Freshman Seminar course and other aspects of the ninth-grade academy (teaming, attendance, and so forth). The organizational facilitator is especially important in a Talent Development High School during the first year to ensure progress through a concrete and focused planning process of the various components. The various aspects of this planning process are presented in Chapters 3 and 5. As we show in Chapter 5, however, the organizational facilitator also may be needed to play a critical role during implementation years to facilitate leadership meetings and ongoing problem solving as the reforms take root. Instructional facilitators, who are often teachers on special assignment from the school district, receive training in using Talent Development curriculum and follow-up with regular coaching support in the classroom with the new approaches and materials.

FROM LISTS TO VISION TO ACTION

The components of the Talent Development model for high school reform are drawn from the pool of available reforms described earlier in this chapter. Indeed, at the level of individual components, there is very little that is new about the Talent Development approach. The power of the Talent Development reform model, rather, rests in the unique way in which it synthesizes multiple reform approaches into a concrete recipe or blueprint that educators may adopt to restructure fundamental features of troubled schools. Through this synthesis, Talent Development moves beyond simply offering a list of good reform principles or ideas. Instead, it provides a comprehensive vision of what an effectively restructured high school that serves all students well can look like, and an implementation process to help schools realize that vision.

Our own experience and study of the experience of other reform ventures have led us to believe that it is important to step forward with both a vision and a blueprint for comprehensive school reform. Educators in low-performing, high-poverty urban high schools work under highly stressful conditions that leave them little time and few resources to invent and follow through with a comprehensive reform agenda, even if they are provided with a facilitated planning process. The Talent Development model provides educators with a concrete blueprint and the support needed to apply that blueprint to their own school. Providing a blueprint for reform should not be confused with a purely top-down approach to reform, however. As we discuss further in Chapter 8, our experiences in the field have led us to articulate a reform approach that strives for a middle ground between a prescriptive, top-down approach and a cocreative approach, thus providing for flexible adaptation to local circumstances and generating the human energy needed for initial and sustained implementation.

No matter how specific and concrete the Talent Development blueprint is, it is of little use to schools unless it works in the real world. As we describe in the next two chapters, the Talent Development approach not only can work in the real world, but actually emerged from (and continues to develop from) a real-world partnership between university-based reform developers and several troubled urban high schools.

PART II

Whole-School High School Restructuring in Baltimore

Chapter 3

Context and Planning for Reform

Even if the thrust of a reform effort is school-based, school reform does not occur in a vacuum. Urban schools are typically part of large bureaucratic systems that involve multiple levels of authority and decision making. This chapter describes the context of the push for high school reform in Baltimore, Maryland. We begin by briefly describing how the nationwide economic and demographic trends reviewed in Chapter 1 played out in Baltimore and contributed to a decline in its comprehensive public high schools which had reached crisis proportions by the early 1990s. We then discuss state- and district-level responses to that crisis, which came in the form of education equity and funding lawsuits, decentralization efforts, and a state reconstitution program. Finally, we turn to the school level, focusing on Patterson High School, with which we were involved through its partnership with Johns Hopkins/CRESPAR, forged during Patterson's planning year for whole-school reform.

IMPACT OF ECONOMIC AND DEMOGRAPHIC CHANGE ON BALTIMORE PUBLIC SCHOOLS

The post-World War II period brought dramatic economic and demographic change to Baltimore City. Before and during the war, the growth of local manufacturing—Bethlehem Steel, the port shipyards, and the airplane industry—had brought prosperity to the city and attracted many new residents, particularly working class Whites and African Americans in search of economic opportunity.

As in many large industrial cities, however, the number of manufacturing jobs in Baltimore declined drastically in the post-World War II decades, dropping from 127,000 in the early 1950s to 44,000 by 1990, with declines continuing through the 1990s. The extensive downsizing of Bethlehem Steel in the early 1980s marked the official end of an era when blue-collar workers with little education could earn enough to support stable lower-middle-class households. To make matters worse, job declines were seen not only in manual labor jobs in steel, shipbuilding, and transportation, but in retail as well. While 80% of all retail sales in Maryland were located in Baltimore in 1950, only 18% of retail sales were located in the city by 1992, with the bulk of retail establishments, and jobs, moving to the rapidly growing outlying suburbs (Orr, 1999).

Suburban development accompanied a dramatic drop in Baltimore's residential population, from nearly a million residents in 1950 to fewer than 650,000 in 1990—a decline of nearly a third (32%). While the overall population decreased, however, the African-American population nearly doubled from 1950 to 1980. From 1950 to 2000, Baltimore's population went from 24% to 64% African American, while the White population decreased by 72%. These data indicate a typical "White flight" pattern that occurred in many cities during this time, reaching its height in the 1970s, in which primarily White middle-class residents moved out of the city and into the rapidly growing suburbs. These changes were accompanied by a shift in the school-age population, with the number of White school-age children decreasing by approximately 76%, while the number of Black school-age children rose by over 100% (U.S. Census Bureau, 2000).

The economic and demographic changes described above resulted in an increased concentration of poverty in Baltimore. By 1990, one in six families in Baltimore fell below the poverty level, three times the state average. One-third of school-age children lived below the poverty line. In 1992, of all districts in Maryland, Baltimore had the greatest number of schools (58%) with 45% or more poor children. Baltimore also was the only district to have schools with 90 to 100% of students living in or near poverty (Orr, 1999).

As we outlined in Chapter 1, the higher concentration of poverty in Baltimore has contributed to other trends that describe the experience of the city's high school-age residents. Baltimore's rate of teen births, for example, has been relatively high. In 1989, nearly one in ten girls 15–17 years old gave birth—three times the national average and five times that of adjacent counties. In 2000, Baltimore's average dropout rate was 10.4%, compared with only 3.9% statewide. City students have continually scored lower than students in the rest of the state on basic functional tests in reading and mathematics instituted by the state in 1989. In 1997, Baltimore City Public School System's [BCPSS] high school students averaged a score of 832 on the SAT compared with a statewide average of 1,014 and a national average of 1,016. The gap can be attributed to students attending the neighborhood high schools; students in the citywide magnet schools scored at or above the state and national averages. Also in 1995, only a third of BCPSS graduates completed the University of Maryland system requirements for entrance into a 4-year college, compared with 51% statewide.

In an economy that offers few employment opportunities for high school dropouts or students who have not gained basic literacy and numeracy skills, these trends have only served to perpetuate the concentration of poverty in Baltimore. As Orr (1999) writes:

> The sheer size and concentration of the misery in the city of the 1980s and 1990s presented the school system with an unprecedented challenge. Never before, in so many schools in the system, had so large a portion of the student population come from such conditions of economic and social havoc. The result was full-fledged crisis in the BCPSS. (p. 71)

STATE AND DISTRICT RESPONSES

The decline of Baltimore public schools by the late 1980s coincided with an era of unprecedented state-level activism to promote educational improvement and reform in Maryland. In 1989, a report released by the governor-appointed Sondheim Commission called for a comprehensive school performance and accountability system to include, among other measures, state-level performance assessments, school report cards, and recommendations that failing schools be "reconstituted" or taken over by the state.

The Baltimore political and education establishment responded to the state's new performance assessment system with concerns that a history of inadequate funding for the district put Baltimore schools at a disadvantage, especially in light of the challenges the district faced serving the majority of the state's poor children. In 1992, the city agreed to join the ACLU in a lawsuit against the state over school funding. Mayor Kurt Schmoke agreed to drop the city's support of the suit, however, when the governor appointed a commission to study and make recommendations to the state legislature to change funding for Baltimore schools. In its final report, the Hutchinson Commission recommended a substantial increase in state funds for BCPSS totaling $500 million over 5 years, to begin in 1994. Fierce opposition by legislators from wealthier suburban counties that had been hit by the recession of the early 1990s, however, derailed the commission recommendations, leaving the issue of funding for Baltimore schools unresolved (Orr, 1999).

At the same time that Baltimore was lobbying for increased funding, an independent study commissioned by the Associated Black Charities at the request of an African-American Baltimore state delegate was released. The Cresap Study (named for the firm that conducted the study) focused on BCPSS management and found much to criticize. Indeed, the report identified numerous personnel problems ranging from incompetence among top administrators, a reliance on personal relationships over experience and performance in promotion decisions, and a general "culture of complacency" that severely limited innovation and effective management. A central recommendation of this study was the implementation of an "enterprise school" system in BCPSS, a form of site-based management that would give building-level administrators greater control over budget and hiring decisions. This and other recommendations that required significant overhaul of BCPSS personnel and financial practices were mandated in the 1994 state budget bill with the provision that state education officials together with BCPSS administrators would monitor their implementation for 3 years. By the next budget cycle, however, legislators expressed disappointment in what they perceived as BCPSS's unwillingness to implement the recommended reforms. They passed a withholding provision to the 1996 state budget that made release of a portion of Baltimore's state education aid contingent on BCPSS's reduction of salaries of administrators who had failed to implement the Cresap reforms (Orr, 1999).

The city-state conflict over education reform and funding reached its climax when Baltimore's Mayor Schmoke filed suit against the state to provide adequate funding to Baltimore schools, release the funding it was withholding, and keep the state from asserting more control over the city's schools through its reconstitution measures. In response, the state countersued, arguing that BCPSS was equally responsible for poor education in Baltimore due to its management problems. With the issues brought to a head and a long legal battle pending, both parties negotiated a settlement that increased state aid to BCPSS in exchange for increased participation by the state in control and management of the city's schools. Increased control came in the form of a restructured school board jointly appointed by the governor and mayor, replacing the superintendent position with a three-person management team made up of a Chief Executive Officer, Chief Academic Officer, and Chief Financial Officer, as well as a commitment to developing a Master Plan based on reforms proposed in the Cresap study. The terms of the consent decree agreement were passed by the legislature and signed into law in April 1997.

RECONSTITUTION

While the city and state were embroiled in the political and legal battles described above, the state began to move forward with the Sondheim Commission's recommendation to take over or "reconstitute" low-performing schools. In this, Maryland has been part of a nationwide trend. The past decade has seen increased efforts on the part of state education authorities to generate improvements in low-performing school districts. While many states have developed performance standards and assessment tools, a growing number have passed laws allowing them to take control of low-performing schools and districts. In 1999, *Education Week* reported that 23 states have passed such legislation, and that about 11 states have actually initiated takeover action in some districts ("State Agencies Take Hands-On Role in Reform," 1999).

Maryland's reconstitution policy was put in place in 1994. Under this policy, the Maryland State Department of Education (MSDE) identified two high schools in Baltimore as "reconstitution eligible." This meant that the schools had up to 3 years to develop and implement a reform plan that would produce concrete improvements on a number of indicators including dropout and promotion rates, and student performance on state functional tests. To support planning and implementation, the state provided some additional funds (at least for initial schools) and special license to transfer and hire staff. Since 1994, Maryland's list of reconstitution eligible schools has grown to 96, 83 of which are in Baltimore. Of the eight large, comprehensive neighborhood high schools, all but one have been identified as reconstitution eligible.

Partially in response to the state's drive for increased oversight of school improvement, a district-level high school reform planning council, chaired by the BCPSS Associate Superintendent for instruction, issued a report in December 1995 outlining plans for high school reform. The plan called for setting common standards for high school graduates, restructuring the neighborhood high schools into small learning communities, with professional development, technology integration, and supports for students' transition to career and postsecondary education. While this plan existed on paper, the turmoil and transition that began that year as result of the state-district tensions made it virtually impossible to implement. The associate superintendent who had spearheaded the report retired by the spring of 1996, and the superintendent was replaced in June 1997, leaving a leadership vacuum at the district level for support. Schools, especially those identified as eligible for reconstitution early on, found themselves very much on their own to plan and implement reforms.

In spring of 1994, Patterson High School was named reconstitution eligible, becoming one of the first two high schools in Maryland to be threatened with takeover if it failed to improve. The following section recounts the events of the critical planning year Patterson embarked upon during the 1994–95 school year, resulting in a radical transformation of the school's organizational structure and academic culture.

RESTRUCTURING PATTERSON HIGH SCHOOL: THE PLANNING YEAR

Background

There is no doubt that Patterson was in great need of some kind of reform. Located in industrial southeast Baltimore, Patterson had felt the effects of increased unemployment and consequent poverty that have plagued many working-class city neighborhoods over the past 2 decades. In the early 1970s, Patterson was known as one of the better neighborhood high schools. Since then, its plummeting achievement, high dropout rates, and increasing truancy and violence earned Patterson a reputation for being academically weak, disorderly, and rough.

When the school was named reconstitution eligible in the spring of 1994, then superintendent Walter Amprey entered into negotiations with the Hyde School, a private boarding school in Maine that proposed to take over management of Patterson. Students, parents, teachers, and union officials vehemently opposed this plan. A particular bone of contention was that all teachers would have to recompete for their jobs under the Hyde plan—a move sanctioned by the state as part of the school's reconstitution eligible status. Students staged a boycott of classes, and parents and teachers protested that the proposal represented an attempt to privatize Patterson, violating the public spirit of the school that had served the community for so long. Confronted with this unwelcome reception, Amprey discontinued negotiations with the Hyde School and instructed school improvement leaders to investigate other reform models, including one being developed at Harlem Park Middle School in Baltimore.

The reform model at Harlem Park was developed in partnership with Education Alternatives, Inc. (EAI, now known as Tesseract Group, Inc.), a private education firm brought in by Amprey to revitalize ailing schools. The model called for breaking up the school into four career magnet programs that operated as separate schools-within-a-school. Excitement around this model and its positive impact on school climate at Harlem Park led to discussions about how it might be implemented at the high school level, and specifically at Patterson. At the end of the 1993–94 school year, Superintendent Amprey recruited an experienced and charismatic assistant principal from Harlem Park to serve as principal at Patterson. She, in turn, recruited several key members of the Harlem Park staff to join her at Patterson, including the magnet coordinator who had been trained by EAI in all aspects of the school-within-a-school approach.

Patterson's new principal and her team had their work cut out for them. In the fall of 1994, the school barely resembled a school. Our site visits revealed a learning environment in chaos due to a very advanced hall culture. Groups of unruly students were roaming the halls and stairways with such frequency that visitors had difficulty distinguishing between when classes were passing and when students were supposed to be in class. Teachers were extremely frustrated with this situation and had essentially retreated to their classrooms where they tried to do their best with the few students who actually came to class. They kept the doors of their rooms closed and locked, and many papered over their door windows to shut out the outside confusion. In a climate survey we conducted in the spring of 1995, 80% of the faculty agreed or strongly agreed that the school environment was not conducive to learning. Ninety percent said that the faculty was frustrated, and nearly two-thirds described the faculty as divided or isolated from one another.

Patterson's Reform Plan

Over the summer of 1994, Patterson's new principal and a planning team made up of her colleagues from Harlem Park and Patterson administrators began to craft a reform plan. Rather than force changes that fall, the group elected to take the following school year to plan and build support for change. Their work continued into the fall, and they began to make the pitch to the rest of the faculty and staff. The preliminary plan included the following core elements:

- Breaking up the school into smaller, schools-within-a-school. In grades 10–12 all students would now attend one of several smaller, career-focused academies. In the ninth grade, students would attend a self-contained academy. Each academy would be located in a separate part of the school with its own entrance and an administrative team made up of an academy principal and an academy leader. Subject-area departments would continue to exist under the new organization to provide periodic instructional support, but the school would be physically and administratively organized around the academies.
- Reorganizing the schedule from seven 50-minute periods into four extended periods of 90 minutes in length to provide more time for in-depth instruction and flexibility in scheduling and in teaching methods.
- Organizing teachers in the Ninth Grade Success Academy into interdisciplinary teacher teams that would share the same students and have a common 90-minute planning period built into the daily schedule. Each team would have a team leader, a lead teacher with

an additional planning period to coordinate team activities. Some experiments with teaming began in the planning year.

- Creating a Twilight School (which eventually opened during the planning year in January 1995) for severely disruptive students, students returning from incarceration, and students otherwise unable to be successful in day school.
- Releasing students at noon every Wednesday to provide time for academies and teams to meet, plan, and participate in professional development activities.
- Installing computer labs, classroom phones, and other state-of-the-art equipment to upgrade the school's technology and communication systems.

Politics and Partnerships

Though the school would not again face the kinds of protests inspired by the Hyde proposal, the process of developing and implementing the new plan was not free from its own political struggles. A small group of Patterson faculty and parents attempted to paint the principal and her team as a group of "outsiders" with little right to come in and propose such sweeping changes. There also was residual concern among the faculty that the new principal would follow the Hyde proposal and force everyone to recompete for their jobs, selecting only those individuals who demonstrated support for the reform program. The principal, in fact, did not opt for that approach. In addition to voluntary transfers and retirements, she requested administrative transfers for only five faculty members—three teachers and two department heads who did not support the reform model. Some young new teachers were hired, and a few teachers who had expressed interest were recruited from neighboring schools to come to Patterson.

Another feature of Patterson's reform plan that created some political waves was a partnership forged between Patterson and the high school reform program based at the Johns Hopkins Center for Social Organization of Schools. The state required all reconstitution-eligible schools to find a local university partner to support their planning and implementation processes. Coincidentally, Patterson had begun its planning process just as the Hopkins group received funding for a new initiative, the Center for Research on the Education of Students Placed At Risk (CRESPAR). One of CRESPAR's core programs focused specifically on urban high school reform, and as the Center's researchers and developers, we welcomed the opportunity to support Patterson's restructuring process. CRESPAR officially partnered with Patterson in January 1995, mid-way through the planning year.

The group already resistant to the principal's plan criticized the partnership as yet another unwelcome intrusion. They caricatured CRESPAR's high school program director as a tyrannical Napoleon figure invading Patterson with lofty but unrealistic reform ideas. It quickly became clear, however, that the principal and her school-based team were driving the reform effort while the CRESPAR partners played only an advisory and support role. The persistent presence of CRESPAR, combined with a willingness to remain in the background, was critical to the ability of the school-based reform team to continue to generate enthusiasm and ownership of the reform process among the majority of Patterson's faculty, staff, and parents. Compared to the widespread resistance to the Hyde proposal, the protest group resisting the reforms was very small. Its lack of a viable counter proposal and failure to garner substantial support among the rest of the faculty and staff at Patterson weakened it further, clearing the way for forward movement with the principal's plan.

Generating Ownership through Collective Planning and Choice

Once the reform planning team settled on the multiple academy model for the school, they invited faculty members to submit specific ideas for types of career academies they would like to help create. Several veteran department heads and teachers came forward not only with ideas, but with a palpable level of enthusiasm and desire to see their ideas implemented.

Eight proposals for career academies were initially offered. Over the course of several meetings, the core planning team worked to decide on the right number of academies for the school and which academy ideas, or combination of ideas, should ultimately be adopted. The proposals were assessed on several criteria, including the strength of preexisting programs in the schools (e.g., business, sports, and automotive technology); faculty and student interests; and information about the local labor market, emerging job opportunities for youth, and potential industry partners for the academies. The group emerged with four concrete career academy themes resulting from a blending of the original proposals: Arts and Humanities; Sports Studies and Health/Wellness; Business and Finance; and Transportation and Engineering Technology. Ninth graders would attend a self-contained Ninth Grade Success Academy.

The process of generating and concretizing academy ideas not only resulted in a more specified reform plan, but also led to a natural expansion of the core team to include the department heads and teacher leaders who had come forward with the academy ideas. Allowing the emergence of this tier of teacher leadership was a critical step in garnering the buy-in and participation of the whole faculty. It was these teacher leaders who invited the whole faculty to begin participating in preliminary planning groups to further flesh out academy mission statements, curricular pathways, and ideas for learning activities and community/industry partners.

Meanwhile, the principal started to decentralize her administrative staff. Patterson was built in such a way that the administrative offices were located in a separate building linked to the rest of the school by an enclosed footbridge. During the planning year, the principal had counselors and assistant principals set up offices in different parts of the instructional wing of the school to make them more visible, accessible, and on hand to manage any problems that arose during the school day. The planning team eventually decided to decentralize all administrative, support, and guidance staff so that each academy could function as much as possible as a relatively autonomous school-within-a-school. They drew up a new organizational chart reflecting the new structure and the various support committees (see Figure 3.1).

Faculty Academy Selection and Placement. As the preliminary planning groups were formed, it became clear that certain types of teachers gravitated toward particular academies. Many English and social studies teachers, for example, wanted to work with the Arts and Humanities group while math teachers gravitated toward the Business and Finance Academy. This was problematic because each academy would need a full complement of math, English, science, and social studies teachers as well as appropriate elective teachers. The problem was addressed in two ways. First, the teacher leaders on the core planning team (now called Academy Leaders) did a fair amount of politicking behind the scenes in an effort to convince teachers they wanted to work with to join their academy. Second, the planning team explained the situation to the faculty and asked faculty to rank order their academy preferences on a selection form. Faculty were also asked to include on the form whether they had any certification in other subject areas and specific skills or reasons why they thought they should be placed in a particular academy.

The planning group used this information to construct teams of faculty and staff for each academy. They placed teachers and staff in each academy based on their first choices and seniority levels. As it turned out, 83% of the faculty received their first or second choices. The principal and members of the planning team spoke with the few who did not receive their first or second choices to keep potential anger and resentment from festering. By inserting an element of choice into academy assignments, involving teacher leaders in the selection process, and keeping open the lines of communication when grievances arose, the placement process was widely viewed as legitimate by faculty and staff.

Student Academy Selection and Placement. Once new academy groups were formed following the faculty selection process, they turned their attention

FIGURE 3.1. **Patterson High School 1995–96, Organizing for Success**

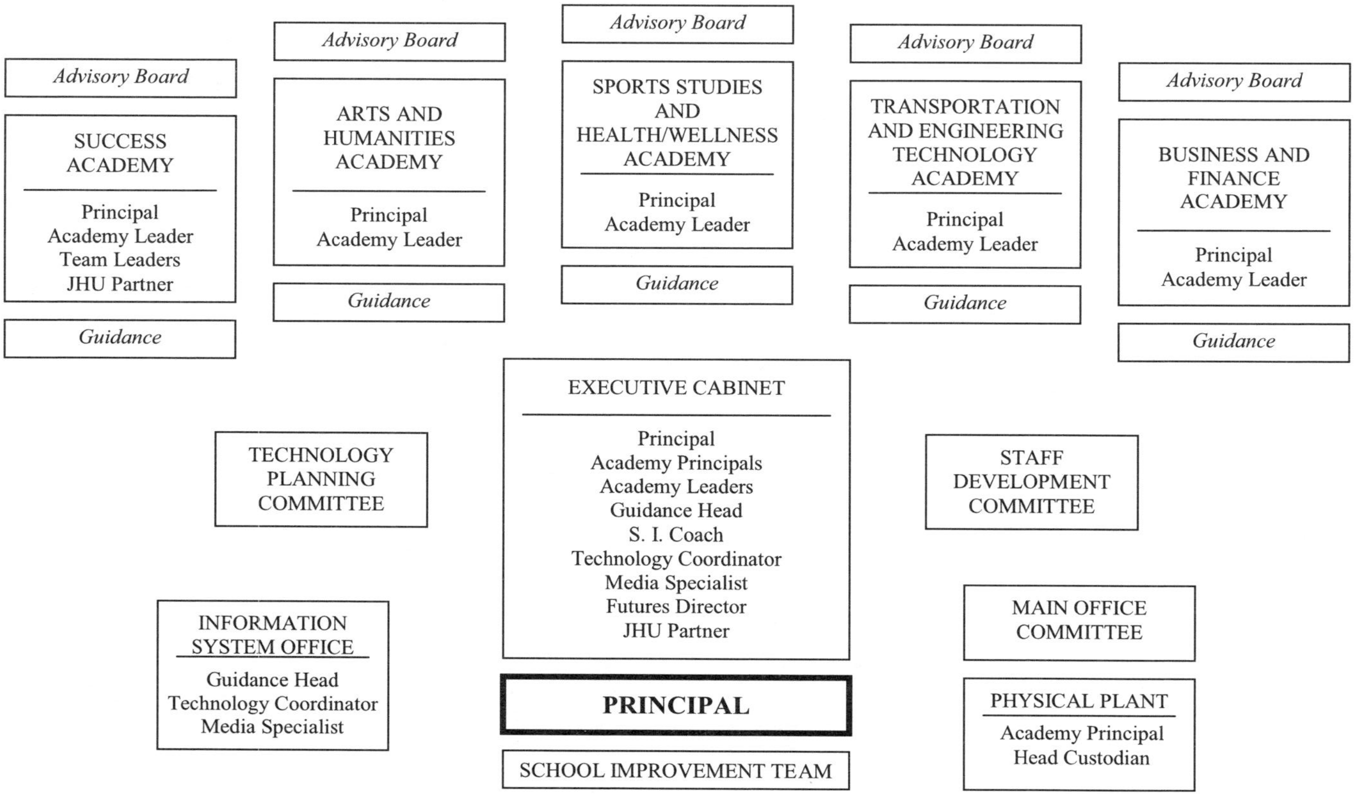

Advisory Board

SUCCESS ACADEMY

Principal
Academy Leader
Team Leaders
JHU Partner

Guidance

Advisory Board

ARTS AND HUMANITIES ACADEMY

Principal
Academy Leader

Guidance

Advisory Board

SPORTS STUDIES AND HEALTH/WELLNESS ACADEMY

Principal
Academy Leader

Guidance

Advisory Board

TRANSPORTATION AND ENGINEERING TECHNOLOGY ACADEMY

Principal
Academy Leader

Guidance

Advisory Board

BUSINESS AND FINANCE ACADEMY

Principal
Academy Leader

Guidance

TECHNOLOGY PLANNING COMMITTEE

EXECUTIVE CABINET

Principal
Academy Principals
Academy Leaders
Guidance Head
S. I. Coach
Technology Coordinator
Media Specialist
Futures Director
JHU Partner

STAFF DEVELOPMENT COMMITTEE

INFORMATION SYSTEM OFFICE

Guidance Head
Technology Coordinator
Media Specialist

PRINCIPAL

SCHOOL IMPROVEMENT TEAM

MAIN OFFICE COMMITTEE

PHYSICAL PLANT

Academy Principal
Head Custodian

to preparing for the student selection process. The planning team had learned that one of the ways in which the academy model supports student engagement is by allowing students to choose their academy, encouraging a level of student commitment to their school program not found in a traditional high school structure. The team was committed to allowing students as much voice as possible in their academy placements.

Academy groups developed brochures and creative assembly presentations to inform students about each academy. They hung signs on school walls and spoke with students in the halls to generate excitement and anticipation and emphasize the importance of academy selection. Letters were sent to parents and guardians informing them of the academy choices and encouraging them to discuss the options with their children. Students were further prepared for academy selection by filling out the Holland Career Interest Inventory, a tool that helps students identify potential career areas based on their strengths and interests.

When the day came for students to turn in their applications, it became clear that all the preparation had paid off. Students were lined up at the doors by 5:00 a.m. with applications in hand (academy placements were to be made on a first come, first served basis). Once placements were made, most students received either their first or second choice. Academy leaders sent out letters welcoming students into their academy, and held special events to give students a chance to tour their academy area and meet the teachers and administrators they would be working with in the coming year. These activities went a long way toward generating enthusiasm and a sense among students and staff that the school was really changing.

The Nitty Gritty

Following faculty and student placement in the new academies, the planning team faced many tasks essential to making the new structure work. These included making changes in the facilities, staffing, and scheduling, and addressing many other operational issues. Much of this work took place in late spring and throughout the summer of the 1994–95 planning year.

Facilities Changes. Organizing Patterson into five separate schools-within-a-school meant identifying adequate space for each academy in the existing school building. The core planning team delegated the task of space reorganization to a smaller subcommittee of teachers and administrators. This turned out to be no mean task. The group had to figure out not only where each academy should be located and identify separate entrances for each, it also had to deal with challenging structural and political issues.

Walls and doors, for example, needed to be installed in various locations to keep the academies self-contained and to ensure adequate classroom and office space, an unanticipated budget item. Ideally, each academy would offer its own science courses, but typical of the traditional departmentalized structure, most of the rooms equipped with water and gas lines needed for labs were located in one part of the building. Finally, a number of teachers at Patterson had occupied the same classroom for upwards of 10 and, in a few cases, even 15 years. Convincing these teachers to move required a reasonable amount of diplomacy and salesmanship. With considerable ingenuity and negotiation, the group was able to devise a plan that required 103 of 104 teachers to move. To everyone's relief, the plan worked and, when moving day arrived at the end of the school year, everyone pitched in to take the next very concrete step toward creating the new Patterson.

A team of people worked during the summer to oversee other facilities changes and continue planning for the fall. Computer labs were installed in different parts of the building, and rooms were equipped for science labs in the Ninth Grade Academy. Phones with outside lines were installed in each academy office and teacher workroom. In the fall, a more flexible public address system was installed to provide every classroom with an internal phone, enabling both schoolwide and academy-specific communication. Attractive professional signs were hung above each academy entrance and directional signs were hung throughout the building. Some academy leaders and teachers worked over the summer to decorate their academy spaces with bright posters and slogans to create a welcoming and inspirational atmosphere. Other changes required considerable creativity; when the team had trouble getting all of the walls built that were needed to separate academy spaces, they set up filing cabinets and other barriers to fill in until the permanent structures could be put in place.

Staffing and Scheduling. As hard as they were, facilities changes at Patterson seemed straightforward compared with the challenges the planning team faced when they got down to the business of scheduling students and staffing the new multiacademy structure. To ensure that teachers did not have too many different classes to prepare, each career academy needed at least two teachers in each core subject area; the Ninth Grade Academy needed a greater number because of its large size. It became apparent very quickly that the wall-to-wall academy structure and four-period day schedule with 90-minute blocks for classes would be very labor intensive (see Canady & Rettig, 1995, for more information on block scheduling). More teachers would need to be hired—not an easy task for a reconstitution-eligible high school in an urban area where qualified teachers, especially

in math and science, are notoriously scarce. Administrative support staff for each academy also needed to be found. During the summer prior to implementation, a great deal of time was spent interviewing prospective teachers and aides for these positions. Funding these positions was also a challenge, since the extra funding Patterson received from the state as a reconstitution-eligible school could not be used for staffing. The principal and the planning team redistributed existing resources and accessed the principal's discretionary fund to support the new positions. They also planned for courses to be offered in Saturday and after-school (Flex School) programs for students who did not pass a course the first time to ensure there would be enough teacher time available to teach academic and academy courses during the regular school day.

Meanwhile, administrative staff began scheduling students in the multiacademy structure. Often cited as the most challenging aspect of the wall-to-wall academy approach, scheduling was no less difficult at Patterson. In years past under the traditional structure, one or two administrators could sit in a room with a computer and generate teacher and student schedules relatively quickly. Scheduling the new Patterson, however, required a more collaborative process. Administrators met with each academy leader to determine which courses would be taught in each academy. Uncertainties about staffing, however, made it difficult to tell until the last minute whether a particular course could be offered in a given academy. Moreover, advanced courses such as Calculus and Journalism, and special courses such as Yearbook could not be offered in each academy because of the limited number of teachers with the qualifications to teach those courses. Much negotiation was required to prioritize courses and determine who would and could ultimately teach which course and where the course would be taught.

The first time around, the most nightmarish aspect of scheduling the new Patterson was purely technical. While block scheduling the ninth-grade teams was relatively straightforward, scheduling the upper-grade students was very challenging. Initial efforts to use existing scheduling software failed repeatedly. As the first day of school drew closer, the schedulers were forced to abandon their computers and schedule each student by hand. Using a large peg board and working well into the night, they finally managed to generate schedules for each student just before school opened. Manuals and technical assistance have since been developed, but as part of the vanguard, Patterson staff did not have access to that assistance at the time.

Other Summer Work. While some members of the planning team were working on facilities changes, staffing, and scheduling, others convened

groups of teachers and staff to hash out details regarding many questions about the new structure that remained to be addressed, such as discipline policy (e.g., which infractions would be handled by the teacher, which by the academy, and which by the school); academy budgets; faculty supervision and evaluation in the absence of department heads in some subjects; where subject-area textbooks and materials would be located and who would have access to them; how students would travel through other academies to reach common facilities such as the cafeteria and the gymnasium; and a professional development plan for the coming year.

The groups tackled many of these issues with the understanding that their solutions would be provisional and subject to revision as they were tested out during the school year. It was decided, for example, that most disciplinary action would take place at the academy level, referring only the most serious infractions to the whole-school principal. As the school year got underway, however, the Ninth Grade Academy principal and leader found themselves swamped with disciplinary problems. They decided to devolve the responsibility even further, giving team leaders in the academy the authority to remove students from class and even, temporarily, from school for certain transgressions.

Budgeting was also designed to preserve academy integrity and empower academy leaders. While the whole-school principal maintained ultimate authority and responsibility for how funds were spent, she was able to give each academy a small budget to support special activities and purchase incentives for students. The Ninth Grade Academy used some of its funds to open an academy store that provided school supplies and nutritious snacks.

One of the stickiest challenges was fulfilling the functions of subject-area department heads (teacher supervision, distribution of supplies, attending district-level meetings, and so forth) in the absence of a departmental structure. The principal and the planning team decided to identify subject-area coordinators to manage supply distribution and facilitate monthly subject-area meetings (many, but not all, of these coordinators were former department heads). Books and supplies would be centrally located and accessible through the coordinator. Each subject-area group could decide collegially who would attend district-level meetings; some groups decided to rotate the responsibility, while others identified a volunteer teacher to attend regularly and report back. Academy leaders were given the primary responsibility for daily supervision of all teachers in their academy, but were able to call upon subject coordinators or other senior teachers for advice and expertise. Academy principals and the whole-school principal retained responsibility for formal teacher evaluations.

Determined to eliminate the rowdy hall culture that had been so destructive to Patterson's learning environment, the planning team focused on how students would move through the building to reach the gym and cafeteria. Of primary concern were ninth graders, who had the furthest to go to reach these locations and who were known to be the least disciplined age group. In meetings over the summer, the leader of the Ninth Grade Academy along with the team leaders devised a plan whereby team leaders and teachers would escort classes of ninth graders through the building. Teachers would also be asked to join the academy leader in watching over ninth-grade students in the cafeteria on a rotating basis.

A final piece of summer work involved planning professional development activities for the coming year. As noted earlier, part of the overall plan was to release students at noon every Wednesday, leaving staff a half day each week for meetings and learning opportunities. With support from CRESPAR, the planning group decided to use this time for three rotating activities: (1) academy meetings every month to provide academy faculty and staff time to address academy issues and troubleshoot; (2) subject-area meetings, facilitated by CRESPAR, focused on developing a common core curriculum for each subject and teaching strategies to most effectively use the 90-minute period; and (3) sessions to build teachers' skills and confidence in the use of computer-based and other instructional technology. The fourth Wednesday would be used for whole-school faculty meetings.

Faculty Retreat. Patterson's planning year culminated in a two-day faculty retreat in late August 1995, just prior to the first day of school. Planned and facilitated in partnership with CRESPAR staff, the retreat was designed to be both informational and inspirational. The whole-school principal began the first day with a motivational presentation that communicated both the structure of the new Patterson and the spirit of community and collective responsibility upon which the structure was based. The faculty and staff then moved into a facilitated team-building exercise, giving the academy groups an opportunity to work together (and compete with other academy groups) in a fun and playful context. The afternoon was spent in workshops, one on interdisciplinary teaming for Ninth Grade Academy faculty, and one on mentoring and advising students for career academy faculty. The day ended with a catered reception on the deck of the boathouse where the retreat was held. Overlooking Baltimore's Inner Harbor, the setting held the metaphor of the Patterson Clipper Ship (the school's mascot) described in the new faculty handbook, "sailing with direction, focus, and the ballast of knowledge, experience, and shared decision-making toward a future of our own design."

On the second day of the retreat, CRESPAR staff presented ways in which the new Patterson exemplified their vision of a Talent Development High

School in which all students were perceived as gifted and talented and received the academic and social support necessary for success. Academy teams then had fun in a contest to develop the best slogans that could be put on academy walls to inspire students to attend school and excel. In another activity, subject-area teachers met to develop plans for encouraging higher passing rates on the Maryland Functional Tests within the academy structure. The final activity was a workshop on use of the 4-period day that gave academy groups time to brainstorm and plan how career academy themes could be blended into the classwork of every subject during the 90-minute period.

The faculty retreat, together with the handbook that was passed out at the retreat, went a long way toward building a sense of common purpose, spirit, and enthusiasm among Patterson's faculty and staff. It ensured that everyone was knowledgeable of the new organizational structure and gave academy groups a chance to begin working together. Finally, for those who had not been actively involved in summer planning, or who were new to the school, the retreat regenerated the momentum for reform that had characterized the previous school year, which was so critical to the successful opening of the new Patterson.

CONCLUSION

As in other manufacturing centers, the economic, demographic, and social changes Baltimore experienced in the post-World War II era had a devastating impact on the city's schools. As Rusk characterized it, the city had become the "region's poorhouse" (quoted in Orr, 1999, p. 80). Faced with the challenge of educating the highest concentration of poor and minority children in the state, it is not surprising that Baltimore leaders were frustrated with the level of resources it was receiving. Given the low performance of many Baltimore schools, it also is not surprising that the state placed pressure on schools to improve and moved to become a more active decision-making presence in the Baltimore public school system.

While the city and state were busy renegotiating their rancorous relationship, however, Patterson High School was moving forward with a reform plan designed to radically transform the school. Uncertainty about funding, about the degree of state authority in local decision making, and about the overall governance structure of BCPSS distracted officials from Patterson's change process. Hence the unprecedented pressure for reform at Patterson was accompanied by minimal state and district oversight, at least initially. In an interesting way, both the pressure and the space this context provided helped galvanize Patterson's new leadership, faculty, and staff, and convince them that if anything was going to change, they were going to have to make it happen. The drive, focus, and energy for change that characterized the planning year at Patterson carried on into the first year of implementation. The initial results of the school's efforts to improve the climate and teaching and learning for students are presented in the next chapter.

Chapter 4

"This Is a Real School Now": Effects of Talent Development Reforms at Patterson High School

The first years of implementing Talent Development reforms at Patterson High School produced many exciting changes. Improvements in climate and interactions among students and adults were immediate and impressive. These changes were eventually accompanied by improvements in attendance and promotion rates over the course of the first year. There were even modest increases in scores on state tests, a rare accomplishment for a school in such an early phase of reform.

In this chapter, we present data from our study of Patterson High School that documents these changes. We begin with an articulation of how Talent Development reforms should affect specific school, student, and faculty/administrator outcomes. We follow with a discussion of the data and methods used to build the base of evidence for the study. The balance of this chapter then presents our findings from the first 2 years of reform implementation at Patterson, supplemented by early evidence from other schools instituting similar reforms.

EXPECTATIONS FOR CHANGE

It is notoriously difficult to accurately "model" the impact of whole-school reform on specific school, staff, and student outcomes. As the previous chapter suggests, whole-school reform takes place in a complex and messy world where multiple layers of political, cultural, and institutional forces; organizational structures; and individual actors collide in often unpredictable ways. It is the worst error of hubris to believe that we, as researchers, can account for all variables that might come into play when trying to explain why particular change occurs in a given school in a particular place at a given point in time. This is especially the case when we serve as both researchers and developers whose interests and actions play a significant role in the shape and implementation of the reforms.

Moreover, whole-school reform by definition does not focus on the manipulation of just one variable—class size or use of a particular curriculum, for example. In contrast, *whole-school* reform is a more *holistic,* even synergistic, enterprise that weaves together multiple reforms of multiple aspects of schooling through a constantly negotiated change process. As such, our ability to claim that a particular reform produces a particular outcome is necessarily limited.

With that said, we nevertheless believe that using a scientific approach to hypothesize expectations for change and to document the extent to which those expectations were, or were not, met is necessary for two reasons. First, and perhaps most important, such research provides schools engaged in whole-school reform with concrete feedback, a critical component of ongoing reflection and improvement. Second, while theorizing and documenting relationships between reforms and outcomes will never produce discovery of a fixed reality or set of causal connections that always hold true regardless of time or place, research can produce understanding, lessons, and guidance for other schools considering similar reforms. Hence, the spirit of this research is concrete and practical. Just as we believe that schools are most likely to change if they are provided with a concrete set of reforms, we also believe that ongoing improvement in schools demands that we articulate a concrete framework for assessing the impact of the reforms and document that impact as best we can along the way.

In general, we expected the Talent Development reforms (described in Chapter 2) to effect positive change in five main areas, as detailed below.

School Climate

Climate is a broad concept that refers to the ways in which students and teachers interact, how safe the school is, and whether the school has a seriousness of purpose as a place of teaching and learning. Schools that are safe, that consistently enforce clear rules and codes of conduct, and where students and adults know one another well and behave respectfully toward one another are considered to have positive climates. In contrast, schools with poor climates are those in which students and adults disrespect each other through abusive language or physical behavior, where students break rules (e.g., cut class, roam halls, curse, or fight) with little consequence, where little learning is taking place, and where adults fail to get to know students and appear to care little about their welfare.

Breaking down a large high school into small learning communities, as called for by the Talent Development approach, should have a positive effect on school climate by making it easier for adults and students to know one another well. The ability to forge more personalized relationships can serve as a deterrent to disrespectful behavior and rule transgression. A smaller group of adults and students may also have a greater opportunity to collectively agree on and maintain their community's rules, creating legitimacy and buy-in. Finally, when adults are responsible for fewer students, they are also more able to enforce rules with greater fairness and consistency.

The specific types of small learning communities recommended by the Talent Development approach can further enhance school climate. The Ninth Grade Success Academy, for example, enables adults to tend to the specific challenges ninth graders face adjusting to high school in an environment free from the distractions and tensions that interaction with older students can present. It also keeps upper-grade career academies from being overwhelmed by the adjustment problems ninth graders bring to school. The career focus of upper-grade career academies, and the fact that students have made a choice to participate in their career academy contribute to maintaining a seriousness of academic purpose in those small learning communities. The Twilight School, as another type of small learning community in the Talent Development model, improves school climate by removing the most unruly and troubled students from the day school environment while, at the same time, providing them with the support they need to reenter day school and/or earn credits toward graduation.

Faculty/Administrator Collaboration

The school-within-a-school organization called for by the Talent Development model can increase collegiality and collaboration among faculty. Small learning communities can provide opportunities for more frequent interactions among staff from different subject areas. Moreover, the focused nature of the Ninth Grade Academy and career academy programs offers staff a sense of common purpose, mission, and goals. Finally, the very process of restructuring a school can increase faculty collaboration as teachers and administrators work together to plan and implement the reforms. Whether such collaboration occurs and is sustained over time, however, depends a great deal on the extent to which it is encouraged by school leaders. Teachers and administrators must have time to work together and be empowered with authority and resources so they can follow through on the plans they make.

Student Attendance

The reasons why so many urban students fail to attend high school on a regular basis are complex and still too poorly understood. However, we hypothesize that Talent Development reforms, and the improvements in school climate that the reforms engender, lead to improvements in student attendance. Students are more likely to attend school if they feel a close connection to adults who show daily concern for their welfare and advancement. Small learning communities also create conditions for adults to share information about students' poor attendance, develop common strategies for encouraging students to come to school regularly, and clearly communicate to students the negative consequences of poor attendance. Finally, more relevant coursework and increased opportunities to experience academic success are likely to draw students to school.

Student Achievement

Students who attend school regularly and who view their schools as serious, relevant, and caring learning environments are likely to achieve more than students who do not. Faculty who work together in small learning communities know their students well, and are better able to communicate and work together to address individual student learning needs. As described in Chapter 2, the Talent Development model also is designed to boost student achievement through curricula that directly addresses poor prior preparation of many urban ninth graders: double doses of English and mathematics in the ninth grade (which pair a special Transition to Advanced Mathematics course with Algebra I and a Strategic Reading course with English I) and the Freshman Seminar course are all geared toward bringing students up to grade level in these important subjects and preparing them for success in the upper grades.

Student Promotion

Students who attend school regularly and who achieve at higher levels are naturally going to be promoted to the next grade at higher rates. This outcome is extremely important since high school students who do not gain promotion to the next grade are likely to become disengaged from school and drop out.

RESEARCH DESIGN

In an ideal research world, participants in our study would have been randomly assigned to treatment and control groups, enabling us to assess the impact of Talent Development reforms while holding other factors constant. Unfortunately, the world of comprehensive school reform is far from ideal, and does not lend itself well to the strict parameters of a true experimental design. We were, however, able to apply a quasiexperimental research design in which data on key outcomes at Patterson following implementation of the reforms were compared to both Patterson baseline data and to data drawn from a school in the same district that closely resembled Patterson. For some outcomes, we compared Patterson to all other large comprehensive high schools in Baltimore to show just how much Patterson came to stand apart as a result of the reforms. This longitudinal and match-control design enabled us to control for as many factors as possible given the limitations placed on us by the real-world context of our study.

To develop as rich a study as possible, we collected and analyzed both quantitative and qualitative data. Quantitative data on student attendance, achievement, and promotion were drawn from school district records spanning the 1993–94 and 1996–97 school years. This gave us data from the year prior to the Talent Development planning year through the second year of implementation at Patterson. Data on school climate and faculty collaboration were collected through student and faculty/staff surveys administered at Patterson and at the match-control school. Baseline data were collected in the spring of 1995, with follow-ups in the fall of 1995, spring of 1996, and spring of 1997. While evidence from Patterson is the centerpiece of this discussion, we use data from other schools that adopted Talent Development reforms in subsequent years to supplement the Patterson story.

While the quantitative data enabled us to assess the overall impact of the reforms, qualitative data collected throughout the study period allowed us to get at the stories behind the numbers. We used ongoing participant observation and focused interviews conducted in the spring of 1996 and spring of 1997 to gain a deeper understanding of how the reforms were being implemented, why they were having an impact, and the areas of tension and struggle that emerged through the implementation process. These data were critical to our ability to report on the details that can make or break a reform effort, which is addressed more thoroughly in Chapter 5.

EFFECTS OF THE REFORMS

Our observations, interviews, and lived experiences as partners in Patterson's reform effort enable us to begin the discussion of our findings with a general description of some of the exciting changes we observed at Patterson during the first years of implementation. We follow that discussion with evidence of the impact of the reforms on school climate, student attendance, promotion, achievement, and staff collaboration in Patterson and other Baltimore high schools implementing Talent Development reforms.

General Observations

When Patterson opened as a "restructured" school in the fall of 1995, positive changes were immediate and palpable. The school was clean, professionally made signs hung above the doors of each academy entrance, and the hallways inside were attractively decorated with welcoming and motivational messages for incoming students. More important, faculty and staff were energized and excited about starting the year in their newly organized school.

The first days of school impressed even those who had been doubtful throughout the reform planning process. Students arriving in the morning spread out to the five different entrances around the building according to the particular academy each was attending. Their own academy principal was at the entrance to greet them each day with a friendly welcome and to check their ID badges. Teachers and students within each career academy and within each team of the ninth grade quickly got to know each other by name. Traffic flow was much more orderly and calm as each smaller group of students moved about their restricted academy space within the larger building. Ninth graders, who tend to be louder and more active than older students, stayed within the Ninth Grade Success Academy, which helped the upper level academies maintain a more mature and relaxed climate.

Implementing the 4-period day at Patterson meant fewer changes of class each day, which cut down passing time in the hallways. Teachers and administrators, energized by the improved climate and more manageable student population, ushered students into their classes in a firm but pleasant way. During class time, students were in class, leaving the halls and stairways clear—a stark contrast to the previous year when so many students roamed the halls that a visitor could not tell whether classes were in session or passing. Teachers taught with their doors open, and the paper that had previously covered the door windows was gone. The attractive seasonal decorations on walls and light fixtures in the halls remained undisturbed by students.

Perhaps most impressive was the strong spirit of reform, openness to learning, helpful attitudes, and a willingness to do extra work that permeated faculty gatherings. Teachers and administrators purchased handsome polo shirts with their own academies' colors and followed a new tradition of wearing them on Thursdays. Similarly, the staff's shared pride and allegiance to Patterson's overall goals and reputation was demonstrated by wearing shirts with the schoolwide colors of blue and white on Fridays. When asked if things had improved, teachers and students responded with: "The improvement is like night and day"; "We have a real school now, not like the playground it used to be"; "I sometimes now feel I've died and gone to teacher's heaven"; and "The school is now 100% better."

Effects on School Climate

Some of the most dramatic evidence of the improvements at Patterson come from survey results about the school climate, based on the questionnaires completed by faculty and students at Patterson and at another large nonselective high school in the district with similar student composition.

Table 4.1 presents teachers' ratings of 12 different potential problems at the school. It shows that much lower percentages of Patterson faculty reported each problem to be serious after the Talent Development reforms than in the year before the changes, when Patterson teachers' reports had looked very much like those of teachers in the comparison school, with

TABLE 4.1. **Percentage of Teachers Rating Each Problem as Serious at Patterson and a Comparison School**

		Patterson	
	Comparison Before *n=92*	*Before* *n=86*	*After* *n=92*
Tardiness	72.2	83.7	17.4
Physical conflicts among students	40.9	45.3	4.3
Vandalism	46.5	64.0	4.3
Absenteeism	92.1	96.5	17.2
Lack of student interest in learning	63.5	67.1	21.1
Use of illegal drugs	63.5	22.6	3.5
Physical abuse of teachers	19.1	21.4	1.1
Verbal abuse of teachers	61.1	65.1	22.6
Lack of student career focus	69.0	57.6	19.8
Class cutting	66.1	84.7	11.8
Lack of student knowledge on college	34.5	29.4	15.4
Teacher absenteeism	17.9	10.8	1.1

TABLE 4.2. **Comparison of Faculty Perceptions from Patterson and a Comparison School**

		Patterson	
School Climate Measure	*Comparison Before*	*Before*	*After*
The learning environment in this school is not conducive to school achievement for most students. (% Disagree)	34.8	20.9	88.0
The level of student misbehavior (e.g., noise, horseplay or fighting in the halls, cafeteria, or student lounge) in this school interferes with my teaching. (% Disagree)	28.8	10.9	70.0
The amount of student tardiness and class cutting in this school interferes with my teaching. (% Disagree)	11.8	14.2	56.3
The attitudes and habits my students bring to class greatly reduce their chances for academic success. (% Disagree)	27.3	29.9	48.8

high percentage reports of serious problems. The improvements are noteworthy in teachers' reports of student deportment (absenteeism, lateness, class cutting, vandalism, and fights), student motivation (interest in learning, career focus, and college awareness), and in relations with teachers (physical and verbal abuse).

Table 4.2 shows equally impressive changes on faculty responses to five statements about school climate. In terms of improvements at Patterson since the reforms and in comparison to a matched school, there is a dramatic flip-flop of previously negative perceptions to positive perceptions. For example, before the reforms, only about 2 of 10 Patterson teachers disagreed with the first negative statement, "The learning environment in this school is not conducive to school achievement for most students." The proportion completely reverses to 8 of 10 after the reforms. Other statements in Table 4.2 show similar patterns and comparisons.

Patterson student surveys show the same strong perceptions of improvements over the 2 years since the Talent Development reforms, in comparison to reports by students at another matched school over the same period. Table 4.3 presents student ratings of improvements in different school characteristics over the period of Talent Development reforms.

The survey responses reflected a change in teachers' and students' ex-

TABLE 4.3. **Percentage of Students Who Report Their School is Somewhat Better or Much Better on Different School Characteristics at Patterson and at a Comparison School**

School Characteristics	*Patterson*	*Comparison School*	*Difference*
Students in halls and stairways who should be in class	61.0	10.1	50.9
Safety in the building	46.4	11.3	35.1
Strict and fair school rules	34.5	8.3	26.2
Bathroom rules	29.7	5.0	24.7
Bathroom appearance	37.7	3.9	33.8
Student behavior in the cafeteria	40.6	12.2	28.4
Your school in comparison to other Baltimore high schools	41.5	10.9	30.6
Your pride in telling others that you go to this school	40.3	24.1	16.2

periences that resulted from specific practices implemented as part of the overall reform strategy. High priority rules and regulations were enforced by staff and followed by students in their small learning communities. Picture ID badges on lanyards with their academy color were issued to every student, and students were required to present them at the academy doorway in the morning and upon entering the cafeteria during the academy lunch period. A student without an ID was required to rent one at 25 cents per day or to buy a replacement for $2. Separate hall passes were needed throughout the day to travel through the building during regular class periods. These practices helped keep students within their own academy space, at their own cafeteria period, and out of the halls when they were not supposed to be there.

Lateness in coming to school resulted in detention after school that day, with the length of detention based on how late the student arrived. Even a few minutes of detention was a hardship because detained students missed the dismissal bus and had to walk a few blocks to get a later bus at a regular public stop. Each academy was able to run a lateness detention program because the numbers of students affected in each academy was manageable and could be consistently enforced each day.

The need for external security officers at Patterson was reduced as a consequence of the reforms. By the school year 1996–97, there was only a single security officer at the school, down from the range of three to seven who had been assigned to the school in earlier years. The single school security officer reported, "Problems such as fights and disruptions are way down this year [1996]. Whereas in previous years the students kept us real busy, I can truly say it's a pleasure to work here now." Students informally interviewed by a visiting U.S. Department of Education official jokingly referred to this officer as "the Maytag man" because he never seemed to have anything to do.

The marked improvement in school safety and discipline at Patterson occurred without suspending as many students as before, because the 50 students who got in the most trouble were sent to the Twilight School from 2:30 to 5:30 in the afternoon to work on their problems and to develop their skills for coping with the structure and demands of high school.

Effects on Attendance

The Ninth Grade Success Academy developed approaches to address the student absenteeism problems that had led to course failures and grade retention in previous years. Teachers who chose the Ninth Grade Academy, some of whom came from middle schools, especially enjoyed working with this age group and realized the crucial importance to students of the transition year into high school. They worked as members of one of five ninth-grade teams of four teachers each, sharing the same students. The ninth-grade staff made good student attendance their top priority. Ninth Grade Success Academy walls were covered with posters about good attendance, recognition of students with excellent attendance for the most recent period, and attendance goals for the future. Each of the five teams of ninth-grade teachers met at least once per week during their common planning time to set attendance goals and to plan ways to reach students with irregular or poor attendance records. Phones were installed so teachers could call students or their parents at home to address absenteeism problems. The teams found that talking directly to the student was most effective for improving attendance, to let students know that someone missed them when they were absent, cared about their coming to school every day, and wanted to help solve the problems that got in the way of good attendance. An expectation that each teacher would make two calls per day produced a steady improvement in ninth-grade attendance.

These efforts paid off. Between 1993–94 and 1996–97, Patterson increased its attendance rate by 10 percentage points for the entire school and by 15 percentage points for its ninth-grade students (see Table 4.4). Over the same period, the average attendance rate in Baltimore's other high schools declined 3 percentage points.

TABLE 4.4. **Percentage of Students in Attendance at Patterson High School Compared with District High School Average (1993–97)**

	Patterson High School					*Rest of School District*					
	9	*10*	*11*	*12*	*Total*	*9*	*10*	*11*	*12*	*Total*	*Difference*
1993–94	61.9	74.9	75.5	82.5	68.8	72.1	77.8	80.8	84.4	76.3	–7.5
Planning Year 1994–95	65.6	76.8	74.8	78.3	70.9	68.6	76.0	78.2	80.9	73.2	–2.3
1st Implementation Year 1995–96	73.6	77.3	81.4	83.2	77.1	66.3	72.8	75.6	79.0	70.4	6.7
2nd Implementation Year 1996–97	77.4	78.0	80.3	83.3	78.9	68.8	75.0	75.6	80.0	73.1	5.8
Difference 1993–94 to 1996–97	15.5	2.5	4.8	0.8	10.1	-3.3	-2.8	-5.2	-4.4	-3.2	13.3

Patterson also saw a large reduction in the percentage of students missing 20 days of school or more (see Table 4.5). In 1993–94, Patterson had the largest percentage of students missing 20 days of school or more among the district's nine nonselective comprehensive high schools. In 1996–97 it had the second lowest rate for all nonselective high schools, with only the smallest high school in the least disadvantaged neighborhood doing better. It was also only one of three schools to see a significant decline in the percentage of students missing 20 days during this period.

Effects on Promotion

Improved attendance at Patterson played a major role in increasing the promotion rate, since students who come to school more regularly are more likely to pass their courses and earn their credits to move on to the next grade. For 1995–96 and 1996–97, only about 15% of 9th graders were repeaters who had been held back the previous year, compared to well over 50% who had repeated 9th grade before the reforms. The 11th graders in 1997–98, the first cohort at Patterson to have experienced the Talent Development reforms since their freshman year, showed a steady increase in the number of students on their way to graduation compared to earlier years. There were nearly twice as many 11th graders in 1997–98 as in

TABLE 4.5. **Percentage of Students Missing 20 Days or More of School (1994–97)**

School	*1993–94*	*1994–95*	*1995–96*	*1996–97*	*Change 1994–97*
Patterson	**74%**	**72%**	**67%**	**64%**	**- 10**
BCHS 1	49%	46%	47%	44%	- 5
BCHS 2	64%	66%	69%	70%	6
BCHS 3	68%	74%	89%	70%	2
BCHS 4	73%	82%	75%	70%	- 3
BCHS 5	73%	72%	72%	72%	- 1
BCHS 6	—	77%	75%	72%	- 5
BCHS 7	73%	75%	77%	74%	- 1
BCHS 8	66%	74%	79%	77%	11
8-school mean	67%	72%	74%	70%	3

Note: BCHS = Baltimore City High School.

TABLE 4.6. **Patterson Enrollment by Grade (1994–98)**

Grade	*1993–94*	*1994–95*	*1995–96*	*1996–97*	*1997–98*
9	1,051	1,208	883	719	771
10	356	407	516	594	577
11	233	246	280	364	424
12	216	235	229	280	313
Total	1,856	2,096	1,908	1,957	2,085

1993–94, before new leadership and Talent Development reforms existed (424 versus 233). The number of juniors and seniors grew by nearly two-thirds over the study period, increasing from 449 in 1993–94 to 737 in 1997–98 (see Table 4.6). As a result, the school was no longer dominated by ninth graders. In the fall of the planning year (1994–95) there were two and a half times as many ninth graders as juniors and seniors. By the fall of 1998, the number of juniors and seniors came close to equaling the number of ninth graders.

In addition to the focus on attendance in the ninth grade, Patterson's after-hours Twilight School program contributed to the higher number of promoted students. About 100 students, mostly ninth graders, wound up in Twilight School for part of the school year. There they took regular academic classes for an 18-week term. They were not allowed to attend classes during the day school. Of the hundred or so students taking classes in the Twilight School, about 30 earned their way back into the regular day school program and did well there. The others remained on the rolls at Twilight School or found placements in other district programs where they could earn a GED credential or combine employment and schooling. One student who had been sent to Twilight School later became an honor roll student in the Transportation and Engineering Technology Academy. In an interview, this student recalled how he "got a counselor" in Twilight School who helped him with his "bad temper," so he "calmed down" and was soon "getting 100s in Algebra" and other courses.

Effects on Achievement

State Functional Tests in core subjects must be passed by every student for a Maryland high school diploma. At Patterson and other nonselective Baltimore high schools, few pass the math or writing tests in the middle grades, so almost all ninth graders are required to take them. During the 1996–97 school year, ninth-grade teachers at Patterson found that the improved climate and increased student attendance made it possible, for the first time in many years, to mount a sustained campaign to improve the pass rate on the State Functional Exams. As shown in Table 4.7, reading scores did not increase. The team did not focus on reading, since over 85% of students pass the reading exam before they come to high school (the proportion who do not pass are typically special education students). The Talent Development High School program also had yet to develop its Strategic Reading course.

The team, with Hopkins's support, did concentrate on improving student performance on the math and writing exams, and their efforts paid off. In 1996–97, Patterson saw a 20 percentage point increase in the number of students passing the mathematics exam and a resumption of the upward trend in the number of students passing the writing exam after a 2-year dip (see Table 4.7).

This gave Patterson the highest pass rate in mathematics among the city's nine neighborhood high schools and the third highest pass rate on the writing exam (see Table 4.8).

School Performance Index

The state of Maryland uses a school performance index based on attendance, retention, and test scores to rate and compare its schools. This in-

TABLE 4.7. **Percentage of Ninth Graders at Patterson Passing Maryland State Functional Exams**

Grade 9	*1993–94*	*1994–95*	*1995–96*	*1996–97*	*Change 1994–97*	*Change 1995–97*
Reading	86%	89%	87%	85%	– 1	– 4
Math	28%	28%	36%	56%	28	+ 28
Writing	55%	44%	45%	57%	2	+ 13

TABLE 4.8. **Percentage of Ninth Graders Passing Maryland State Functional Math and Writing Exams in 1997**

School	*Percentage Passing Math*	*Percentage Passing Writing*
Patterson	**56 %**	**57 %**
BCHS 1	46 %	75 %
BCHS 2	41 %	59 %
BCHS 3	40 %	41 %
BCHS 4	35 %	49 %
BCHS 5	33 %	52 %
BCHS 6	29 %	46 %
BCHS 7	28 %	54 %
BCHS 8	26 %	47 %
8-school mean	34 %	52 %

Note: BCHS = Baltimore City High School.

dex summarizes the elements and progress of the Talent Development High School Model, which focuses on the interrelationship of climate, attendance, promotion, and academic achievement. In 1994–95, Patterson had the second worst school performance index among the nine nonselective comprehensive high schools in Baltimore (see Table 4.9). This is, in part, why it was selected as one of first two high schools in the state to be eligible for reconstitution. By 1996–97, Patterson had the second highest index score among all nonselective comprehensive high schools in the city and the highest rate among the eight largest schools. This significant pro-

TABLE 4.9. **School Performance Index 1995–97**

School	*1995*	*1996*	*1997*	*Change 1995–97*
Patterson	**75.1**	**76.0**	**82.1**	**7.0**
BCHS 1	89.6	87.9	86.9	–2.7
BCHS 2	69.9	68.1	69.9	0.1
BCHS 3	75.2	74.7	73.9	–1.3
BCHS 4	75.4	73.4	78.6	3.2
BCHS 5	75.8	73.4	76.7	0.9
BCHS 6	76.6	75.8	76.1	–0.5
BCHS 7	77.1	74.4	78.8	1.7
BCHS 8	77.7	76.0	74.8	2.9
8–school mean	76.4	74.9	76.0	–0.4

Note: BCHS = Baltimore City High School.

gress occurred during a period of general stagnation for the majority of nonselective comprehensive high schools in Baltimore.

Student withdrawal rates from Patterson have steadily declined since the reforms were introduced (785 in 1994–95, 714 in 1995–96, and 660 in 1996–97), which helps confirm that the improvements in attendance, promotion rates, and test scores were actual upward trends. These improvements cannot be discounted by student attrition or selection bias that would have removed more students over the years who would otherwise have drawn down school means. Patterson produced higher average student outcomes at the same time that it helped more students remain at the school.

Effects on Faculty/Staff Collaboration

We viewed faculty and staff collaboration as a key mechanism through which smaller, more personalized learning environments can have a positive impact on student engagement and learning. Hence, we developed survey items to measure different aspects of teacher-teacher and teacher-administrator relations. The first set of items is drawn from Little's typology of teacher-teacher interactions in schools (Little, 1990). Her research identifies four types of collegial relations among teachers that span a continuum of interdependence: (1) storytelling and informal exchanges; (2) one-on-one aid and assistance; (3) routine sharing of materials, methods, and ideas; and (4) actual joint work in which teachers share responsibility for tasks and organize their time and resources cooperatively. Informal exchanges require the least amount of interdependence, while joint work requires the most.

Analyses show that prior to the reforms, only about half of the teachers at Patterson reported that they engaged in one-on-one assistance often or very often during a typical week. Fewer than half reported frequent informal exchanges or routine sharing, and only one-quarter of the faculty reported engaging in joint work with their colleagues. In contrast, by the end of the first implementation year, the number of teachers who reported frequent informal conversations with their colleagues nearly doubled. The number of teachers engaged in one-on-one assistance and routine sharing also increased substantially. Most satisfying, the number of teachers who reported that they engaged in joint work with their colleagues doubled over the first 2 years of implementation.

Other measures also showed marked improvements in teachers' sense of collaboration and in their perceptions of administrative leadership and support during the first implementation year. Prior to implementation, for example, only a third of teachers described the faculty as cohesive. In contrast, by the end of the first year of reforms, data from our climate survey showed that 80% of the teachers described their faculty as cohesive. The number of teachers who agreed with the statement, "This school seems like a big family; everyone is so close and cordial," rose from a mere 13% prior to the reforms to 67% by the spring of 1996.

The reforms also had a positive impact on faculty perceptions of school administrators during the first year. While only half felt that the school administration's behavior toward staff was supportive and encouraging prior to the reforms, 80% felt this way after the first year of implementation. During the course of the first year, the percentage of faculty who felt that staff received recognition for a job well done rose from 40% to more than 70%. By the end of the first implementation year, Patterson's principal also was perceived by more teachers to be proactive, clear about her vision for the school, sympathetic to problems faced by staff, and likely to enforce school rules and back up teachers.

While the first-year data indicate impressive improvements in levels of teacher collaboration and faculty and staff relations, second-year data show signs that cooperative attitudes and behavior among staff at Patterson began to unravel as the reform process continued. While nearly the entire faculty experienced a sense of shared mission and a great deal of cooperative effort among staff at the end of the first year, fewer than three-quarters of the staff expressed similar opinions by the end of the second year. Similarly, only slightly more than a third of the faculty felt that Patterson seemed "like a big family" after the second year, dropping from more than two-thirds at the end of the first year of the reforms. Moreover, while the principal appeared to retain the faculty's confidence in terms of vision, goals, and openness to innovation, teacher perceptions of overall administrative support diminished. Fewer teachers expressed feeling involved in decision making or characterized administrators as encouraging and in touch with teachers' problems.

SUMMING UP

During the first 2 years of reform, Patterson faculty and administrators worked very hard to implement major changes in their school—a process that not only created a more collegial environment and increased interaction among adults in the school, but which ultimately resulted in significant improvements in school climate and gains in student attendance, promotion, and achievement. Data presented in this chapter shows that Talent Development reforms generated largely positive outcomes for adults and students at Patterson.

For the most part, teacher perceptions of collaboration and administrative leadership and support did not revert to prereform levels. However, declines in the second year point to tensions among school staff that emerged as implementation deepened. These data suggest a great deal of work would have to be done to work out the kinks in the new organizational structure; clarify roles, responsibilities, and lines of authority; and continue to deepen the impact of the reforms. The challenges of this work, the lessons we have learned from it and from our efforts to scale up the reform model to other high schools, are laid out in the following chapters.

PART III

Challenges to Creating Talent Development High Schools

CHAPTER 5

The Devil's in the Details: Lessons Learned from Implementing Talent Development High School Reforms

By all accounts, the first year of implementing the Ninth Grade Academy and career academy at Patterson High School was an exciting success. As we discuss at the end of Chapter 4, however, teachers' sense of collaboration and evaluations of administrative leadership and support declined by the end of the second year of implementation. These declines turned out to be an accurate barometer of social relations among faculty and staff at Patterson as the reform process continued. In this chapter, we show how tensions at Patterson went unattended and eventually built toward a crisis that threatened the entire restructuring effort. Throughout the chapter we point out the critical lessons about implementing whole-school high school reform that we learned along the way.

UNEXPECTED IMPLEMENTATION HURDLES AT PATTERSON

Survey data at the end of the second year of implementing the reforms showed declines in the spirit of cooperation and faculty and staff relations in general at Patterson. Observation and interview data, however, reveal nascent tensions at the end of the first implementation year. From these qualitative data, we have identified several interrelated phenomena that carried over into the second year and strained cooperative reform efforts at Patterson. These included tension between academies (especially between the Ninth Grade Academy and the upper grade academies), the challenges of dealing with multiple authority figures, tensions around the appropriate involvement of the whole-school principal in academy affairs, and the ambiguous nature of academy leaders' and team leaders' authority with respect to classroom teachers.

Inter-Academy Tension

Organizational structures such as teams or schools-within-a-school can encourage collaboration among faculty, but can create divisions as well. As Hargreaves (1994) argues, schools with such structures risk becoming "balkanized," losing the unity and clarity of purpose and goals essential to overall school success. This sense of separation was present at Patterson during the first year of implementation. When asked whether they thought the faculty was cohesive or divided, the following teacher's response was typical:

> Now that's probably one of the most difficult things. Because we are in separate academies, we have actually become separate faculty. And some of the staff members here say that they feel that when they go into another academy, that they're not really a part of Patterson. Like you step from your domain into their domain.

It is unclear whether such divisions are necessarily destructive. Secondary schools have always been complex organizations where teachers are often more involved with a subgroup in the school, such as a subject-area department, than with teachers in other parts of the school (Little & McLaughlin, 1993). Talent Development reforms do not do away with such groupings, but rather replace subject-oriented departments with student-oriented small learning communities that still encourage decentralization of authority and decision making at the academy level. At Patterson, however, tension infused the relationship between the Ninth Grade Academy and the upper grade academies as the separation ultimately reintroduced a status differential between the teachers of older, more mature students and those teaching younger, unruly ninth graders, as the following comments reveal:

> The division that I see this year is the division between the Success Academy faculty and the upper level academy faculty. . . . We're never together. We don't care to be together . . . or, they don't care to be with us. We don't matter to them because we're the ninth grade. It's not a friendly thing. It doesn't feel friendly.

> There's a division between ninth grade success and the other part of the school. They think they're above us, they think they've arrived, they think they're more in a position to do whatever. And all you hear is "those ninth graders."

The school principal inadvertently played a role in creating an unequal division between the ninth-grade teachers and the career academy teachers when, in an effort to give Ninth Grade Academy teachers a pep talk, she told them she believed in "promoting" people, implying that they wouldn't necessarily be "stuck" in the Ninth Grade Academy forever. Though the problem was recognized in the middle of the year and some steps were taken to ameliorate it, administrators' efforts seemed contrived to many teachers:

> I understand that there's a mandate now from [the whole-school principal] saying that all the academies must get together now. We must like each other. So that's going to happen, that's taken care of, that's been mandated. [Laughs]

It became clear that, throughout the first year of implementation, ninth-grade teachers felt very isolated from their colleagues in other academies and that this isolation took on negative psychological and emotional dimensions.

Multiple Authority Figures

Restructuring Patterson into five separate academies resulted in the creation of six relatively autonomous administrative authorities, one for each of the five academies and for the whole school. The Ninth Grade Academy was further divided into teams that were designed to function as even smaller units within the school-within-a-school.

While virtually all teachers and administrators interviewed held positive attitudes toward the new school organization, some tended to qualify their positive responses with expressions of confusion and frustration about exactly who was "in charge." As one ninth-grade teacher exclaimed:

> There are too many things here. You've got your academy leader, your team leader, your floor leader, your principal. Would somebody please tell me who's in charge? Who is the boss? That's what I want to know!

This teacher was uncertain about who had authority to evaluate her teaching, and what the relationship was between the academy administration and her team leader regarding student discipline.

Ninth-grade teachers who taught electives (physical education, art, and so forth) had an especially difficult time knowing whom to turn to for discipline problems, because they had little involvement with any particular team. As one of these teachers clearly stated, "Unfortunately, we don't know who to deal with for discipline. Do we deal with the principal, the team leader, who. . . ?"

Other teachers expressed difficulty in working around conflicts among the administrators of different academies. Several younger teachers had to take students to other parts of the school building to use facilities located in other academies (e.g., the gym, the auditorium). These teachers reported a number of instances in which they were caught in the middle of scheduling and policy conflicts between the Ninth Grade Academy and the academy where the facility was located. Academy leaders had argued over ninth graders disrupting other classes as they passed through other academies to reach the gym, and who should dispense discipline when ninth graders misbehaved in their physical education class—the Ninth Grade Academy leader or the Sports Academy leader.

Teachers whose work spanned the two academies also felt torn between the rules and norms of one academy and the other. For example, the administration of the academy where the gym was located promoted a hard-line, zero-tolerance discipline policy. When ninth-grade students misbehaved or failed to suit up for physical education, the academy administrator expected teachers to send those students back to the Ninth Grade Academy for reprimand. This expectation conflicted with the Ninth Grade Academy administration's efforts to encourage teachers to work with problem students as much as possible rather than immediately ship them off to an administrator.

To resolve these problems, ninth-grade leaders used a flexible scheduling approach. They arranged for their students to take physical education outside during the first and fourth quarters of the school year when the weather was reliably good. During the second and third quarters, students took their health class indoors in the Ninth Grade Academy. With this arrangement, ninth graders did not need to go to the gymnasium at all. Ninth graders still had to travel to the cafeteria, library, and auditorium, however. According to the teachers who reported feeling "stuck in between," the general conflict was never adequately addressed at the administrator level, leaving teachers feeling tense and uncertain of the appropriate action to take when students misbehaved.

Involvement of the Whole-School Principal

Under the new organization at Patterson, teachers had very little daily contact with the whole-school administration. They would go directly to their academy to sign in when they arrived at school in the morning, and left through the academy door at the end of the day. While a few teachers seemed to accept this as a natural outcome of the new organization, a number of teachers were not altogether comfortable with their lack of contact with the whole-school principal. Most expressed this discomfort with some degree of resentment, as if the principal did not care about them or their academy, and as if her presence could help solve some of the academy's problems. When asked how they thought their whole-school administration was doing, these teachers replied with the following statements:

> Well, I don't know. I don't ever hear anything from Ms. P [whole-school principal]. Does she know what we're doing down here? You know what I mean? Does she know what kind of job I'm doing? Does she know . . . that's what my question is, does she?

> Who is she? I mean, I haven't seen her down here once. . . . It's tough for me when you're trying to change a school so much and you seem like you're so into this but then you never see her down here. . . . I would just like her to know what is going on down here. I don't think half the problems would go on down here if she took an interest in them.

These teachers' responses were typical and pointed to a general desire among some teachers for more contact with their whole-school principal.

Not surprisingly, academy administrators did not share the teachers' desire for a larger presence of the whole-school principal in their academy, as exemplified in this exchange with the Ninth Grade Academy principal:

NL: Do you think that [the whole-school principal] should be more visible in the Ninth Grade Academy?

Ms. P: No. In fact I think that she shouldn't be more visible anywhere. Because the reason this is working is the empowerment of the leadership team in each academy. Her presence would disempower those people.

The whole-school principal also felt it was important to resist getting involved in the affairs of any individual academy:

NL: Do you ever catch yourself . . .

Ms. P: Trying to micromanage?

NL: Yes.

Ms. P: Sometimes. Sometimes. And I have to draw back because then that will show folks that you don't have confidence in them and that certainly is something that I don't want to instill. I want them to be able to do it their way as long as the results are what they should be.

While administrators, both at the whole-school and the academy level, were invested in the decentralization principle that undergirded the new organization, classroom teachers continued to perceive the whole-school principal as an important authority figure (a perception not unfounded since she retained the ultimate authority to evaluate and hire and fire) and someone they wished would play a greater role in their work lives.

Ambiguous Authority

As mentioned in Chapter 3, each of the academies at Patterson was staffed by both an academy principal and an academy leader. The academy leader position was designed as a lead teacher role; that is, to provide instructional leadership, coordinate and support subject-area groups within the academy, and ensure that teachers have the instructional materials they need. Academy leaders had difficulty developing the instructional leadership aspects of their position, however. Instead, the academy leaders typically became "second in command" to the academy principal, spending a great deal of time dealing with discipline, hall control, parents, and administrative duties like daily attendance and report cards.

That the academy leader more closely resembled an assistant academy principal than an instructional leader during the first year of reform was due partly to the school's focus on climate control and student attendance rather than to improvements in instruction. Part of the reason why the instructional aspects of the position remained undeveloped, however, was an uncertainty on the parts of both the academy leader and the teachers about how they should relate to one another. In one academy, for example, several teachers expressed confusion when the academy leader made an unannounced visit to their classrooms, since he played no formal role in evaluating them and the informal role he might play had never been clarified. For his part, the academy leader struggled with a position that held responsibility but little real authority over teachers and instructional development:

> My frustration is . . . I haven't discovered yet in this position the authority line, when it comes to handling adult-related problems. I'm not sure, given the nature of what an academy leader means in this setup, that I'll ever fully answer that. I think a lot of it will have to be developed on my own levels of fairness, collegiality, and moral suasion.

Academy leaders found a much less ambiguous role and more concrete lines of authority when they were performing duties as assistant academy principals. Their immersion in those duties left little time to develop the lead teacher role, and as a consequence, teachers viewed them more as administrators than as instructional colleagues. The following year, the whole-school principal attempted to clarify their roles by renaming their positions "academy instructional leaders" and asking them to focus on the quality of teaching in their academy. They continued to be called upon to perform daily administrative duties, however, and were frustrated by the instructional support role they did not feel they had time to fulfill.

Similar to the academy leader, teachers appointed as team leaders to the interdisciplinary teams in the Ninth Grade Academy also struggled with ambiguous authority. Observations and interviews revealed that one of the most significant challenges for team leaders on at least two of the teams was dealing with a "weak link" on the team—that is, a teacher who was unable to manage his or her classroom and problem students effectively. Team leaders on teams with a weak link expressed frustration with this situation, especially when the teacher failed to apply strategies or respond to team efforts to help. One team leader reported that she was consistently interrupted from her own teaching at least three times a day by a weak teacher to "take me out of this room to his room to tell his students what he should be telling them." This team leader felt that the only solution was to increase the power and authority of her position:

> I feel that team leaders should be able to pick the people . . . I think the team leaders should be able to interview the people that are going to be on their team. We should be able to tell whether or not our personalities will mesh together, and if they're not, I think we should be able to dismiss people . . . I'm serious. We should be able to dismiss them when they're not doing what they're supposed to be doing. When I'm a team of four, I shouldn't be a team of three.

Though team leaders were expected to "lead" their teams, they did not possess the power or authority to choose team members or discipline teachers who were not performing up to team standards.

EMERGING DIVISIONS IN YEAR 2

Interacademy tensions and status differences described above were only some of the issues that needed attention at Patterson. However, it became more difficult to address the inevitable growing pains of a reforming high school because a crack was beginning to form in the leadership team. As the second implementation year got underway, tensions among key leaders over such issues as standards and promotion were exacerbated by dwindling finances and the pressures of providing "full inclusion" services to Patterson's special education students. In the following paragraphs we describe these emerging tensions and the devastating consequences they had for Patterson's core leadership team.

Standards and Promotion

One of the main bones of contention among school leaders lay in a debate over standards and promotion policies. During the first year of implementing the reforms at Patterson, career academy leaders set high standards for students. For the most part, the 10th to 12th graders in the academies were able to meet those standards because they were students who had not experienced much academic difficulty; those who had failed the prior year were either retained in the ninth grade or had transferred or dropped out. The Ninth Grade Academy leadership's goal during the first year of implementation was to help as many ninth graders as possible attain the credits they needed to be promoted to the tenth grade. As the data presented in Chapter 4 indicate, they were successful, holding back only 15% of freshmen from entering tenth grade in 1996–97 as compared with over 50% in the previous year.

When these promoted students entered the career academies in the fall of 1996, career academy leaders found themselves facing a much larger tenth-grade class than they had the year before. Moreover, a larger proportion of these tenth graders were students who would have been held back in ninth grade or even dropped out without the efforts of Ninth Grade Academy faculty to provide them with the extra help they needed to pass. A small number of the tenth graders came from Twilight School, the after-school program for students with discipline problems or other life circumstances that kept them from succeeding in the regular day school. The Ninth Grade Academy also implemented a campaign to help ninth-grade repeaters earn the credits they needed during the first term so that they could be promoted at mid-year. Their success meant even more tenth graders for the upper grade academies.

Contending with a larger number of students overall, and more students with academic and discipline problems than they had the previous year, career academy leaders argued that the Ninth Grade Academy's standards were too low and that the academy was promoting ninth graders who should have been retained. Ninth grade leaders argued that the students' success was not due to lower standards but to the motivating, student-centered environment of the Ninth Grade Academy and teachers' efforts to provide them with the extra help they needed to pass their courses. They also claimed that the upper grade academies were taking an elitist and even racist stance toward students, wanting to work only with the best students while avoiding the extra work necessary to help lower-achieving students succeed in school.

Inclusion

The tensions within the leadership team might have been managed through effective facilitation and leadership in the group's weekly meetings. The whole-school principal, however, was distracted by intense district oversight of the special education program and fulfilling the state's meeting and paperwork requirements as a reconstitution-eligible school. In 1996–97, Patterson's second implementation year, the school adopted a "full inclusion" model for most of its special education students. Patterson's primary feeder middle school operated an inclusion model and the administrative team decided to continue this approach for these students when they came to Patterson. "Full inclusion" meant that nearly all special education students would be enrolled in regular education classes supported by the presence of a special education teacher. Ideally, the model would enable special education students to participate in the academy programs rather than being segregated in separate classes in a different part of the school. In fact, there were not nearly enough special education teachers to provide in-class support to all special education students in all of the academies. Inclusion also requires thorough training of both special and regular educators so they can learn to work together effectively. Although training took place, many teachers did not feel that their collaboration with other teachers was well supported or particularly successful.

While special education students who did not have a special education teacher in their classes received support in special resource rooms located in each academy, some parents became concerned that their children were not getting the services they were legally due according to their individual education plans (IEPs). Their complaints quickly drew the attention of district officials who were particularly sensitive about special education services. The district's legal battles with the state (described in Chapter 3) stemmed from a lawsuit in part over special education. The resulting consent decree had laid down specific guidelines for special education compliance. In an effort to avoid further expensive—and politically embarrassing—legal action, district officials began to conduct intensive oversight at Patterson. Oversight included lengthy weekly meetings with the principal that required extensive and time-consuming preparation and paperwork. Knowing that principals had been fired for less in the district, Patterson's principal felt she had no choice but to comply even though she knew it was taking her energy away from leading the continuing reform efforts.

Finances and Resource Distribution

Money weighed heavily on the principal's mind as well. The additional staff, computer labs, facilities changes, new P.A. system, and other improvements to the school during the planning and first implementation years were financed largely through state reconstitution and compensatory education funds. However, unanticipated costs such as wiring and air-conditioning for computer labs, contracting out and eventually hiring new custodial staff, and additional staffing for the academies put the budget in deficit. Patterson was among several high schools that had budget problems during this time, and some individuals we interviewed suggested that the district accounting system was not as efficient or accurate as it should have been. In any case, there was a lack of clarity between the schools and the district accounting office under the new site-based management "enterprise school" system that resulted in confusion about the budget at the school level.

Finances also contributed to divisions among academy leaders. Interview data revealed a general perception among career academy leaders and teachers that the Ninth Grade Academy was receiving a disproportionate amount of resources from the whole-school budget and Johns Hopkins/CRESPAR. It appeared to them that the Ninth Grade Academy had more staff, supplies, training, and funding for motivational materials such as T-shirts and prizes for students than did the career academies. The Ninth Grade Academy leader also was promoted to academy principal, a position for which others on the leadership team felt the individual was not fully qualified.

Consequences of Polarized Leadership

For its part, Johns Hopkins/CRESPAR staff continued to provide instructional and organizational support to Patterson during its second implementation year. As we describe further below, however, Hopkins was assisting other schools in Baltimore by this point and, like Patterson's principal, its staff was distracted and spread thin. Because Patterson's leadership team had been such a cohesive and effective group in the past, there was little precedence for direct intervention and Hopkins staff trusted that the leadership team would be able to work through its differences. Though aware of increasing tensions, Hopkins staff did not fully understand the severity of the situation until it was too late.

By the spring of 1997, the leadership team had become fractured and polarized. Philosophical differences and struggles over fine tuning and deepening the reforms became personal battles. Meetings became extremely tense and unproductive, and some leaders stopped communicating with each other outside of these meetings. The principal began calling meetings that included only her administrative staff (academy principals), leaving out the lead teachers (academy leaders) who had held so much of the spirit of the academies and the reforms during the planning and first implementation years. This had two results. First, the excluded leaders and teachers began to feel less involved in decision making. It appeared that the principal was moving toward a more top-down administrative model of leadership and away from the more inclusive model that characterized earlier stages of the reform process. Second, the academy leaders felt alienated, angry with the principal, and especially resentful of the newly promoted academy principal who had worked with the principal in a previous school and who continued to work closely with her in decision making.

It was this atmosphere of general discontent and frustration with which district officials met when they began a deeper investigation of special education services and general success of the reforms at Patterson in the late spring and summer of 1997. Had there been unequivocal support for the principal and unity among school leaders, investigators may have focused on the overall success of the reforms for students, acknowledged the problems, and moved toward working with the school to solve them. As matters stood, however, it appeared to district officials that the school's principal, and those close to her, were the problem. Indeed, there were rumors that a group of parents and teachers in the school were quietly pressuring district leaders to oust the principal. Even so, it came as a shock to the Patterson community when the school's Area Executive Officer announced the transfer of the principal in late August 1997.

A dramatic school improvement team meeting following announcement of the principal's transfer drew nearly 200 participants and led to an appeal to the school board. By this time, however, a new board had been put in place as a result of the consent decree and an interim chief executive officer had replaced the outgoing superintendent. New to the district and just gaining their footing, the board and CEO were reluctant to overturn a personnel decision made by an incumbent area executive officer; so the board upheld the transfer. Patterson's principal led an alternative middle school program for the 1997–98 school year and then retired after 35 years of service. The ninth-grade principal left Patterson as well, and the district turned the school over to one of the assistant principals to serve on an interim basis until a permanent replacement could be found.

These events took the wind out of the reform sails at Patterson. Contrary to expectations, a principal hired to replace the interim principal stayed only through the end of the 1997–98 school year when he left to take a position at a suburban high school. In the Ninth Grade Academy, the loss of the leaders who had created the program caused climate and morale to deteriorate, eroding the attendance and achievement gains of the previous 2 years. Disillusioned with the reform effort, key academy leaders eventually left to take other positions, leaving career academies without the individuals whose vision and work had created the academies. As the fourth new principal in 5 years arrived at Patterson in the fall of 1998, the future of the school and its reform efforts appeared very uncertain.

LESSONS FROM PATTERSON

While there are many lessons that can be derived from the first 2 years of implementing reforms at Patterson, we focus on the following four as especially critical.

Lesson 1: High schools adopting Talent Development reforms must work to balance academy autonomy with a common commitment to whole-school reform.

The Talent Development model, with its Ninth Grade Academy and upper grade career academies, can reinforce traditional status differences between teachers teaching younger and those teaching older students. At Patterson, this was overlaid with philosophical tensions around issues of standards and promotion, and resentment over perceived inequalities in the distribution of resources among academies. While competition among academies in this model can help stimulate innovation, creativity, and hard work, it also can create potentially damaging divisions that may ultimately undermine the overall reform effort. Avoiding this pitfall requires leadership, open communication, and constant recommitment to the success of all students served by the school; hence Lesson 2.

Lesson 2: Structural reforms in themselves do not turn around a failing school.

Structural reforms create opportunities for more personal interaction, positive engagement, and the development of a culture conducive to teaching and learning. The ultimate effectiveness of these reforms, however, depends on sustained human effort, attention, commitment, communication, and creativity.

The leadership team of a multiacademy school must be committed to collectively struggling through the inevitable challenges of whole-school reform. As often occurs in the initial phase of many human partnerships,

Patterson's leadership team experienced the tremendous excitement, cohesion, creativity, and commitment required to revitalize the school. The momentum and desire for change naturally ebbed, however, when the school began living the reforms on a daily basis. This tendency for a change process to become quieter and for a new organizational structure to become more routinized is healthy to the extent that it enables individuals to relax into relatively stable roles and responsibilities and focus on doing their jobs. A healthy organization, however, sustains a mechanism, typically some form of leadership council, for addressing problems that arise through daily practice and for continuously improving the reforms. If this team is committed, able to communicate openly, define problems and generate short- and long-term solutions, realize that uncomfortable struggle is part of the process, and agree to respectfully disagree when necessary, then it has a chance of sustaining and improving the reform effort.

If key leaders become distracted and exhausted, however, and if the group is continually frustrated with the lack of easily found solutions and unresolved issues, then the unhealthy dynamics of blame, judgment, polarized views, and loss of commitment to the overall mission can occur. In this context, it is easy for leaders to abandon collective decision making and fall back on a more top-down administrative approach that excludes perceived troublemakers. While in the short run this may make decision making less of a struggle (and may be an appropriate approach for some individual decisions), if it becomes systemic practice, it can fracture the organization and weaken the legitimacy of its leaders.

The time that is required to lead a multiacademy school and an effective leadership team means that the whole-school principal must be buffered from too many outside distractions. In a multiacademy school, a good deal of administrative authority is delegated to academy-level leadership. This structure does not make the whole-school principal's job any easier, however. As we argued earlier, the autonomous identity of each academy, and competition among them, must be balanced by a strong commitment to the success of all students in the school. The whole-school principal must constantly reinforce this commitment through a visible presence throughout the school and ongoing engagement in inter- and intra-academy problem solving. By "engagement" we do not mean micromanagement, but rather a supportive attentiveness that inspires and energizes faculty and students to succeed. Whole-school principals must be available to facilitate communication, offer creative suggestions, validate solutions, and, at times, assert the authority needed to make difficult decisions.

These critical duties are difficult to perform if the principal is continually pulled away from the daily operation of the school. Certainly a principal's job is complex and multifaceted. But district and state officials can contribute to principals' exhaustion and sense of being overwhelmed by requiring excessive paperwork and by being insensitive to the amount of time and energy needed to run a school well. In Patterson's case, the principal was both distracted and demoralized by the intensive and punitive way in which the district asserted oversight of the special education program. She also spent considerable time responding to state reconstitution monitors' requirements for extensive planning and reporting documentation. The experience of Patterson's principal, and others with whom we have worked, strongly suggests that the top-down bureaucratic management approach of district and state authorities is ill suited to the needs of a reforming high school and its principal.

Lesson 3: A leadership team in a reforming high school must be supported through its struggles by the district and other outside reform partners.

On-site presence of reform facilitators must be sustained. Even the healthiest leadership teams can get stuck on problems that seem to have no solution, or in a polarized argument that undermines the team's commitment and effectiveness. In these cases, external reform partners may be able to assist the team. District or state partners, for example, may be able to remove barriers to decision making by waiving curriculum or staffing requirements that stand in the way. University-based partners may be able to provide information, training, resources, or research to help resolve an issue. Consistent presence of outside partners in leadership meetings may help add perspective, reminding the group of its successes and overall mission in moments when it seems mired down in a difficult problem. Partners also may come in and help facilitate key meetings to help the team move beyond a sticking point and return to a more productive problem-solving mode.

The role of outside reform partners in education is complex and not very well theorized. On the one hand, we have found that the constant presence of a reform facilitator is important to introducing and effectively planning whole-school reform. School teams cannot be expected simultaneously to run a school and plan for major restructuring without help. However, an external reform partner must not be overly identified with a school's reform effort; the reforms discussed here can work only if they are owned and driven by school-based leaders and staff and not overly dependent on an external presence for implementation. There is a general sense in the reform community that the need for external support should wither away to allow a school to sustain implementation on its own. We argue that while intensive outside support is critical for the planning and initial implementation phases, assistance from external partners may need to be continued for an indefinite period to help negotiate inevitable changes in district policy, leadership, and other potentially disruptive forces. Sustaining school-partner relationships requires a strong commitment on both sides.

Lesson 4: District leaders must adopt a broad and long-term perspective when assessing problems in a reforming school, and make decisions in ways that support and sustain rather than destabilize reform efforts.

Patterson's experience highlights three aspects of this lesson:

- *Adequate resources are important to the success of whole-school reform.* Whole-school restructuring cannot be done on a shoestring budget. We encourage schools to critically examine their budgets and shift resources to support reform implementation. Additional resources are required, however, especially at the outset, for facilities changes, professional development/planning time, and staffing. Unfortunately, we have found that the amount of financial and human resources available to urban high schools is often unclear. In Baltimore, enrollment levels projected in the spring determine high school budgets for the following school year. By the middle of October, however, schools are to calculate their actual enrollment and then either receive additional funding for students over the projection, or refund the system if they have fewer students than projected. This is not such a problem for citywide magnet high schools that have some ability to control their enrollment through selection. It is a nightmare for the nonselective high schools, however, which face much higher levels of student mobility. For these schools to improve, they must be able to plan, and effective planning requires a certain level of certainty and stability. Losing tens of thousands of dollars halfway through the first term in a school year forces principals either to eliminate teaching positions (and thereby disrupt student learning mid-term) or, alternatively, gut budgets for building improvements, technology, or even basic supplies for day-to-day operation. An equally bad situation occurs in high schools that are underfunded for the first 2 months of school. They find themselves understaffed, overwhelmed by students, and often unable to recover from a chaotic school opening. In addition to addressing yearly uncertainties in the regular school budget, schools also require additional funding to pay for the costs of reform, especially at the outset. At Patterson, many of these costs were supported through Title I Compensatory Education funds and State Reconstitution funds. Unanticipated costs and additional staffing needs, however, drove the school into deficit.

• *Special education must be managed creatively with district support in a multi-academy school.* As Patterson's experience shows, it is not easy to structure special education programs so that all students can benefit from the academy programs and receive the services to which they are legally entitled. In large, urban, nonmagnet public high schools, it is not unusual for a quarter of the student body to be involved in the special education system. Special education is often the largest "department" in such schools. Patterson's move toward a full-inclusion approach was right in line with cutting-edge special education philosophy and tenets of Talent Development. In retrospect, Patterson may have moved too quickly. Full inclusion requires extensive training in cooperative teaching, on-site support, and enough staff to ensure adequate service delivery. On the other side, however, Patterson's experience also demonstrates the need to insert greater flexibility in the special education system for reforming schools. Using computer-assisted learning, for example, can improve students' skills and provide important exposure to technology while reducing the number of faculty needed to provide services. Critical reviews of IEPs may also help to identify students who can be transitioned out of special education and into regular classes with minimal support. In any case, districts must be aware of the need to be creative with special education programs and actively support reforming schools to provide services without undermining the reform process.

• *Leadership changes, especially, must be conducted with great care.* Unfortunately, the lack of a high-level champion for high school reform within the central district office in Baltimore (see Chapter 3) created a context in which quickly fixing what was perceived as a personnel crisis took priority over doing what was best for the overall reform effort at Patterson. Transferring a principal in a reforming high school, especially one who has led the original reform team, must include a great deal of thought, planning, and preparation. Ideally, a principal's successor would be selected carefully and participate in a training period before taking charge of the school. Removing a principal in late August with little advanced warning solves few problems, and creates a crisis atmosphere that can undermine reforms.

SUSTAINING REFORM AT PATTERSON

Student outcome data from the 1997–98 school year reveals the negative affects of the upheaval at Patterson. The annual dropout rate, which had declined dramatically, from over 19% in spring 1996 to 9.5% by spring 1997 (the second year of TDHS implementation), rose again to just under

14% by the spring of 1998. Though 9th grade passing rates on the Maryland Functional Writing Test rose slightly, rates on the math test plummeted from 56% in spring 1997 to 40% in spring 1998. While schoolwide attendance had risen to 79% by spring 1997, it dropped 5 percentage points to 74% the following year. The School Performance Index (the weighted summary measure of student achievement, attendance, and dropout rates) showed Patterson declining from a high of 82 in spring 1997 to 77 by the end of 1998.

Happily, these negative trends did not continue. Leadership at Patterson finally stabilized by the 1998–99 school year with the arrival of a new principal who still occupies the position to date. The new principal was chosen in part because she had worked in high school-level school-to-careers education. She made a strong commitment to sustaining and strengthening Patterson's career academies from the outset. The career academies have continued to provide students with academic- and career-focused instruction in self-contained small learning communities. The Ninth Grade Academy has struggled, however. Leadership and faculty turnover and a move away from the teaming model have made it difficult for the academy to recreate the supportive, student-centered environment that characterized the initial years of its implementation.

Patterson's data improved during the 1998–99 and 1999–2000 school years. Its School Performance Index increased to nearly 83 by spring 1999, and jumped to 90 by spring 2000, indicating gains in attendance, achievement, and lowering dropout rates.

Most impressive, a longitudinal analysis of student data shows that the strong Ninth Grade Academy in the first years of implementation combined with the improving career academies to support increased student success. Mac Iver, Legters, and Durham (in press) analyzed dropout and graduation rates for two cohorts of Patterson students, the class of 1998 and the class of 2000. Figure 5.1 shows that of the students who were freshmen in fall 1994 (the class of 1998), 63% dropped out, 12% were still in school, and 18% graduated 4 years later. If one can take a breath and move beyond the outraged gasp elicited by a 63% cohort dropout rate, note that Figure 5.1 shows significant improvements for the class of 2000 cohort, where only 45% dropped out and 27% graduated. Recall that the class of 2000 at Patterson were freshman during the 1996–97 school year, the second implementation year of TDHS reforms. These students benefitted from a highly supportive Ninth Grade Academy experience and continued on in 10th to12th grades in one of the improving career-focused small learning communities. A slightly larger proportion of the class of 2000 went on to a 2- or 4-year college than in past years. More strikingly, 82% of

FIGURE 5.1. (Source: R.E. Durham, special tabulation, September, 12, 2001)

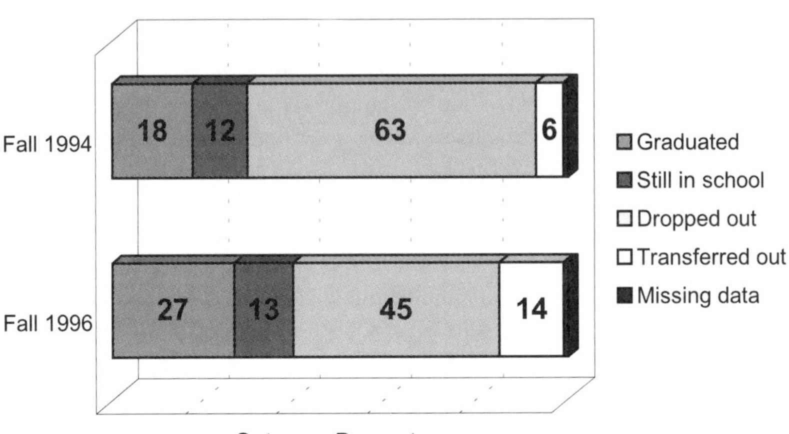

these students completed the course requirements for entry into the University of Maryland, compared with a previous high of 47% in 1997.

Though a 45% cohort dropout rate implies much room for improvement, Patterson has been successful in keeping a greater proportion of this group of students in school and on track for graduation than in prior years. Comparative data show that Patterson's 18 percentage point drop in its dropout rate and 9 percentage point increase in its graduation rate across these two cohorts represents greater improvements than in any of the eight neighborhood comprehensive high schools in Baltimore. These data provide strong evidence that Patterson's restructuring made a difference in the lives of the students who benefitted from 4 years of relatively high implementation of TDHS reforms. Future data will tell whether subsequent cohorts continue these upward trends at Patterson.

CONCLUSION

The partnership between Patterson and Johns Hopkins/CRESPAR has gradually receded since the 1997–98 school year. The contentious politics surrounding the leadership transition made it difficult to recreate with new school leaders the close relationship that had been forged by Talent Development staff and members of the team that led the initial restructuring effort. Patterson still welcomes visiting groups led by Hopkins Talent Development staff, and Hopkins remains available as a partner when needs arise, but TDHS facilitators no longer maintain an active presence in the school.

Patterson's example, early success, and the sustained presence of the TDHS reform model in the school inspired other high schools to embark on a similar reform path. Many of these schools approached Johns Hopkins/CRESPAR for assistance. In the next chapter, we describe the steps, and missteps, of our efforts to support expansion of the Patterson Talent Development model to troubled high schools in Baltimore and Philadelphia.

CHAPTER 6

The Story Continues: Early Scale-Up Efforts in Baltimore and Philadelphia

In the introduction to her book *Common Purpose,* Lisbeth Schorr (1997) writes of programs designed to address serious social problems. "[W]e have learned to create the small exceptions that can change the lives of hundreds. But we have not learned how to make the exceptions the rule to change the lives of millions" (p. x). As Schorr goes on to demonstrate, "scaling-up," or expanding to a large number of settings a small program that has been successful in one or in a small number of settings, has been one of the most daunting challenges of reform. Schorr offers positive examples of programs that have succeeded in reaching a socially meaningful scale, yet much of the impetus of her book lies in the troubling fact that so many other promising programs are not sustained or expanded.

The 1990s saw developers of a growing number of comprehensive school reform designs attempt to move beyond their pilot sites to serve a greater number of districts and schools. It is still too early to tell whether these efforts will ultimately be successful. Initial studies, however, are generating a wealth of information about comprehensive school reform and suggest some common elements of successful scaling-up efforts. These elements include adequate resources, alignment of commitment, standards, and assessment among all levels of the system (community, school, district, and state), capacity of design teams to provide support, creation of support networks among teachers within and among schools, a focus on teaching and learning (not just on school structures), and a restructuring model that is clear and practical enough to be implemented yet flexible enough to adapt to varying local contexts (Bodilly, 1998; Bodilly & Berends, 1999; Stringfield & Datnow, 1998).

In this chapter and the next, we share our experiences of scaling-up the Talent Development High School model in Baltimore and Philadelphia. These experiences generated numerous practical lessons about planning, implementation, and contextual factors that we hope will contribute to the growing knowledge base on scaling-up comprehensive reform models.

INITIAL SCALE-UP IN BALTIMORE

In late spring and summer of 1996, following Patterson's impressive first implementation year, several other Baltimore high schools expressed a strong desire to move forward with the same restructuring plan. Under reconstitution pressure from the state, three of these schools decided to attempt full implementation of the Ninth Grade Academy and the career academies in the fall of 1996. Another school, not yet identified as eligible for reconstitution, decided to take the 1996–97 school year to plan its academies and begin full implementation in the fall of 1997. All four schools asked Hopkins/CRESPAR for support.

For the three schools attempting restructuring after only a few months of planning, it soon became clear that fast-track implementation was a dangerous path. Academy concepts were created quickly, leaving little time to build faculty buy-in or develop new ideas that might be more relevant to students' interests and needs. Not anticipating such early and rapid scale-up, the Hopkins staff became spread thin and had not yet developed the organizational and curricular tools needed to support the implementation of the reforms. Each school attempted teacher and student selection processes, but many teachers found when they came to school in late August that their assignments had been changed due to massive problems with staffing and scheduling. Students and teachers were confused about the physical boundaries of the academies. Though students had an official academy affiliation, their identification with their academy was weakened when they found themselves taking classes throughout the school and from teachers outside of their academy, instead of primarily in a designated academy space with dedicated academy teachers. To many, it appeared that the academies were, at best, a realignment of preexisting programs or, at worst, nominal fictions existing in name only. Moreover, because of the lack of faculty involvement in the initial planning, there was little energy to address the problems as the school year progressed. Chaotic school openings due to scheduling and space problems gave faculty and students the sense that the reforms had failed before they had even begun.

In contrast to the fast-track schools, restructuring went more smoothly at the fourth school that took an entire year to plan. A team of administrators and faculty at this school had begun working on academy themes the prior spring with support from a school district facilitator. By fall, the team was ready to form academy working groups around the themes and welcome faculty members to step forward with additional concepts. A strong principal was joined by a half-time facilitator from Hopkins/CRESPAR to keep the planning process moving forward. Following the Patterson model, a steering committee was formed that determined final academy concepts and oversaw the faculty academy selection and placement process, the marketing of academies to students, and the student selection and placement process. The steering committee also formed a building committee early on to work on dividing the building into separate schools-within-a-school. With the aid of a volunteer architect who helped draw up the plans, the building committee was able to present a plan to the faculty in time for everyone to make the necessary moves at the end of the school year. The principal identified academy principals and leaders early on, leaving time during the planning year to develop initial curricular pathways for each academy, decide what courses should be offered in the Ninth Grade Academy, and build a sense of teamwork and academy identity among faculty.

With the groundwork laid, this fourth school opened in the fall of 1997 with academies that were much more real and energized than in the other schools that had taken much less time to plan. Staffing and scheduling were a challenge for this school, however. Administrators new to scheduling were assigned to create the schedule for the academy structure. Though they had coaching from Patterson schedulers, staffing constraints and the lack of computer software combined to make the task extremely difficult. Hence, the schedule produced for the fall term was not "clean" in the sense that some teachers were required to teach students outside of their academy. The school minimized student movement as much as possible, however, by asking teachers to move to another classroom for the period outside their academy. The steering committee also continued to meet as a leadership council during the first implementation year, enabling schedulers, academy principals, and academy leaders to discuss and improve the schedule for the second term.

LESSONS LEARNED FROM EARLY SCALE-UP IN BALTIMORE

These examples demonstrate that whole-school, high school restructuring requires much more than a set of ideas or even committed leadership. We found that reforms take hold only when schools take the time to engage in a collective planning process that respects, and provides time to work through, the complex human and technical aspects of such a dramatic change effort. The following lessons describe these aspects in more detail.

Lesson 5: Planning time is essential for effective implementation of Talent Development reforms.

• *Planning time allows leadership to emerge and a new form of governance to take hold.* Transforming a failing high school requires calling everything into question, including the leadership structure. Under traditional high school organization, leadership roles typically include the principal, assistant principals with various schoolwide duties, and subject-area department heads. A schoolwide schools-within-a-school or academy structure calls for different roles, including academy principals capable of running their own small school-within-a-school, and academy leaders who assist with administration in the academy and provide collegial leadership and support to all teachers in the academy regardless of subject area. In some cases, existing assistant principals and department heads demonstrate the leadership skills, energy, and vision needed to transition well into academy principal and leader roles. In other cases, existing leaders may lack the energy and enthusiasm for reform and may even feel threatened and resistant to change. We found that taking a year to plan enabled schools to work through the politics of leadership to create a stronger, more invested group of leaders who held more legitimacy in the eyes of the faculty than in schools that planned only for a few months. In the schools that took a year to plan, there was time to win over assistant principals and department heads who were talented leaders but initially resistant to change. Indeed, these individuals were important to the planning process because they often played devil's advocate, pointing out potential problem areas that needed to be addressed. Perhaps more important, there was time for other leaders to emerge from the teaching faculty—individuals with energy and good ideas who were able to step forward and prove their leadership qualities in planning meetings and other reform activities. At Patterson, there was also time and license to identify and transfer existing leaders whose resistance to change was so steadfast that remaining in a leadership position would be detrimental to overall reform efforts. The other school that took a year to plan was restricted in its ability to do this and was forced to sustain "weak links" in its leadership team. The three fast-track schools had absolutely no opportunity to allow new leaders to emerge or really work through the resistance of existing leaders, weakening their ability to implement the reforms.

• *Planning time is required to achieve collective ownership of reforms.* At Patterson and the replication sites in Baltimore, achieving a strong initial implementation of schoolwide reforms required much more than simple agreement among faculty and staff to a new vision for the school. We found that the importance of adequate planning time lay in the opportunity it afforded to engage the entire faculty in the actual work of generating initial academy concepts, settling on actual academies for the school, marketing academies to students, determining and designing academy space, and fleshing out ideas for courses and activities for each academy. In the schools that took an entire year to plan, there was time for the meetings, discussions, assemblies, and other activities needed to accomplish this work collectively. Over time, that work built a sense of pride and ownership of the reforms among faculty and staff, creating a stronger implementation and a more positive climate for the inevitable problem solving that would be needed once the school began living the reforms. In the fast-track schools, a small group of primarily administrators and CRESPAR staff made many of the key decisions from the top down, leaving most of the faculty disinvested of the reform process.

• *Planning time is needed to create academies that serve all students equally.* Tracking is a fundamental feature of traditional high school organization and culture. The tendency to track students is so strong that we have found it resurfacing even in schools committed to implementing a common core curriculum and a multiacademy structure designed to support advancement for all students. Schools must guard against creating some academies for college-bound students while relegating other students to more vocationally oriented or general "catch-all" academies with lower academic standards. In the early Baltimore scale-up effort, we found that such imbalances among academies occurred to a greater extent in fast-track schools.

• *Planning time is necessary to work through difficult technical aspects of schoolwide reform.* This early experience of scaling-up in Baltimore also underscored the critical importance of staffing, scheduling, facilities changes, and other concrete markers of distinct academy identities to successful implementation. A full planning year gives schools time to assess their school building, and determine the best configuration for a multiacademy school. Academy boundaries, entrances, traffic flow, classrooms, office space, bathrooms, and lab facilities can all be thought through and needed changes can be made to make the academies as self-contained as possible.

Early assessment of staffing needs is also critical to implementing true schools-within-a-school. Ideally, each academy should have enough math, English, science, and social studies teachers to teach all the students in its academy. Early planning allows principals and leadership teams to identify gaps in their staffing models and where they may have surplus positions (e.g., in physical education or special education departments), and to begin shifting resources and hiring accordingly. Doing some of this during the school year, as opposed to the summer, is helpful because faculty members may know reform-minded peers in other schools or finishing teacher certification programs who might be recruited. There also need to be enough administrators and support staff for each academy. In the Baltimore scale-up school that took an entire year to plan, an additional assistant principal was hired to run one of the academies. In the other schools, some assistant principals had to become academy principals for two academies, dividing their time and attention and detracting from the self-contained aspect.

By all accounts, scheduling is one of the most important technical aspects of a multiacademy school. A "clean" schedule where teachers and students remain in their academies for the majority of their classes and activities enables staff and students to develop close relationships, forge a strong academy identity, and reinforce a sense of community. In addition to being one of the most important technical aspects of creating a wall-to-wall academy school, scheduling also is probably the most difficult. This is due in part to the fact that schools often lack adequate staffing. Lack of training and computer software is equally to blame, however. In many ways, all of the early implementation schools in Baltimore were victims of being the vanguard and none was able to develop a completely "clean" schedule with no student or teacher crossing of academies. Patterson and the other school that took an entire year to plan, however, approximated this ideal much more closely than did the fast-track schools. Under so much time pressure and lacking adequate tools, the three fast-track schools fell back on traditional methods and created schedules that weakened the self-contained ideal of their academies.

Lesson 6: Consistent, on-site facilitation is important for planning and implementation.

Though mentioned above, this bears repeating. At Patterson, Hopkins/CRESPAR staff was consistently present throughout the planning and first implementation year. Though not without its ups and downs, this consistency enabled the development of a relationship between the partners that was generally characterized by mutual trust and goodwill. Moreover, as the first Talent Development site, the reform model developed at Patterson was a true co-creation, combining the vision and ideas of both partners. Hopkins/CRESPAR staff did not need to be concerned that Patterson would be stalled or sidetracked in moments when they were not present because the model was truly in the minds and hearts and daily activities of Patterson's core planning team.

Matters were different in the replication sites. Enamored of Patterson's success and under pressure from the state to reform rapidly, the three fast-track schools turned to Hopkins/CRESPAR for assistance. Because the schools were "importing" a model developed elsewhere, they relied on Hopkins/CRESPAR to provide the vision, plans, and leadership to a greater extent than at Patterson. Principals and other leaders at these schools also were so busy running their schools and writing reconstitution plans for the state, they relied on Hopkins/CRESPAR to actually facilitate much of the planning. Hopkins/CRESPAR, however, was inadequately staffed to support four schools, and had yet to develop the necessary tools to provide the intensive on-site facilitation needed to keep the schools on track. As one CRESPAR facilitator stated, "A lot can happen in a week" to undermine the planning process if the facilitator is not present at the school. All of these factors, combined with the enormous time pressure, made planning and implementation frustrating for all involved.

Realizing the need for more intensive facilitation, Hopkins/CRESPAR assigned a half-time organizational facilitator to the Baltimore school that decided to take an entire year to plan. The combination of a dedicated facilitator focused on this one school, a strong principal who understood the basic elements of the model, and an entire year to plan made implementation at this school stronger.

EARLY WORK IN PHILADELPHIA

By the spring of 1997, news of Patterson's reform efforts and the Talent Development Model was spreading beyond Baltimore. News articles appeared in the *Baltimore Sun, Education Week*, and *Educational Leadership* describing the reforms and lauding Patterson's early success. Patterson and some of the other Baltimore high schools began receiving visitors from other schools and school systems interested in implementing similar reforms.

Olney High School in Philadelphia was one of the first schools outside of Baltimore to express interest in the Talent Development model. Like Patterson, Olney had been known as a good school but had experienced a chronic drop in academic performance and overall climate over the previous two decades. Declines were so severe that Philadelphia's superintendent invoked the "keystone" provision in the teachers' contract in February 1997. Akin to reconstitution in Maryland, the keystone process gave the district the power to make changes to improve a school if student achievement fell below the district's standard. Most notably, the keystone process allowed the district to transfer and replace up to 75% of a school's faculty ("Hornbeck's Fix for Two Ailing Schools: New Faculties," 1997).

Students demonstrated for 3 straight days against the naming of Olney and Audenreid, another Philadelphia high school, as "keystoned" schools. The district also found itself in a legal battle with the Philadelphia teachers' union. In 1994, the Philadelphia Federation of Teachers had agreed to include the keystone process in the contract as long as union officials were involved in the identification of schools to be keystoned and staff to be terminated or transferred. A breakdown in communication had occurred while identifying the schools, however, and union officials felt that the superintendent had moved forward without their participation. The union ultimately sued the district to block implementation at Olney and Audenreid.

Meanwhile, a reform-minded principal assigned to Olney in fall 1996 was eager to make dramatic changes. Previously an elementary and middle school principal, she had worked with Johns Hopkins education programs in the past and was interested in adopting the Talent Development model. She began negotiations with Hopkins/CRESPAR in spring 1997 to begin a fast-track planning process so that the school could reopen the following fall with at least the organizational reforms (academies and extended class period) in place.

A planning process that involved the faculty was virtually impossible, however, after Olney was keystoned. Faculty did not know whether they would be returning to the school in the fall, and many suspected that the new principal had asked the superintendent to keystone the school so she could replace them with new staff. Relations between the principal and much of the faculty became even more rancorous when several teachers' cars were searched for school property near the last day of school. The principal found herself moving forward with lukewarm support from only a few administrators and faculty members. Planning for Talent Development reforms continued through the summer, but the atmosphere of uncertainty made decisions difficult, and the plan was never infused in the hearts and minds of the Olney faculty.

In mid-summer 1997, a labor arbitrator ruled in favor of the teachers' union, allowing teachers at Olney and Audenreid to keep their present assignments. Though nearly a third elected to transfer out anyway, the ruling meant that faculty hostile to the principal would be returning to Olney. In addition, the principal was scrambling in late summer to find new teachers to fill the empty slots. Scheduling was a nightmare, and the school experienced a chaotic opening in the fall, with few teachers or students understanding or fully supporting the new organization. The superintendent ultimately decided to remove the principal in early fall, realizing that negative relations between the principal and faculty were blocking improvements at Olney. The reform process at Olney continued, but it would be some time before the school recovered and took a more positive direction.

Lesson 7: District- and school-level union leaders must be involved and supportive of the reform process.

In addition to the pitfalls of a fast-track planning process, an obvious lesson from this initial reform effort at Olney is the importance of local teacher union support. Talent Development reforms especially call for a tremendous collective effort during the planning period. This was impossible to achieve at Olney given the battle over keystoning between the district administration and the union, especially because at issue was not just a contract, but also teachers' actual job assignments. Principals who have been most successful in implementing Talent Development reforms have done so in a context of relatively smooth relations between the district and union at the district level. These principals also respect the union presence in their buildings by including building representatives on the reform planning team.

Lesson 8: Positive relations between principal and faculty are necessary for productive planning and implementation of whole-school reform.

While most of the Olney faculty actually supported the Talent Development reform concept, their mistrust of the new principal and fear, uncertainty, and anger over the keystoning process was a major barrier to reform. As the Patterson case showed, opposition of a few faculty members can typically be overcome through a careful planning process. A positive, inclusive attitude, a reform vision, a leadership team respected by the faculty, and no public battles between the district administration and the teachers' union made it possible for Patterson's principal to move forward without alienating the majority of her faculty. From the outset, Olney's principal had difficulty establishing good relations with the faculty. The public nature of the keystone process and the fact that it was perceived by teachers, and their union, as a top-down administrative fiat, further deepened the divisions. Under such conditions, it was impossible to create the support and momentum required to effectively plan and implement whole-school reform.

Literature on school reform and effective schools cites the critical importance of a strong principal to provide the vision, leadership, and management for reforming schools. Much of this research focuses on elementary and middle schools, however. While a strong principal is certainly important, our early experience in Philadelphia and in other schools suggests that the "lone rider" approach is ineffective in the face of whole-school reform at the high school level. Most public high schools are large organizations with large faculties, making it impossible for the principal to develop close personal relationships with everyone on her staff or monitor the implementation of reforms in every part of the building. High schools also are typically organized into smaller subunits such as departments or small learning communities, requiring a much greater delegation of power and responsibility to other administrators and teachers than in a smaller school. Moreover, high school teachers have a reputation for being more politicized than middle or elementary school teachers and less likely to comply if they disagree with a principal's plans.

All of this means that effective leadership for whole-school reform at the high school level requires a team approach. Principals must create a leadership team, ideally comprised of both administrators and lead teachers, to tend to all of the human, political, and technical aspects of planning and implementing whole-school reform. As we argued in the Patterson context, the cohesiveness of this team, and its ability to struggle through difficult challenges, is extremely important and can make or break a reform effort.

SUSTAINING REFORM IN BALTIMORE

Compared to the first 2 years at Patterson, the four other high schools in Baltimore achieved relatively weak implementations of the Talent Development model. The three fast-track schools continued to be plagued by staffing and scheduling problems and never got their career academies functioning as true schools-within-a-school. Largely excluded from the planning process, faculty were not energized enough to make the reforms come alive. In the school that took a year to plan, career academies were implemented and grew well for 2 years. The Ninth Grade Academy, however, split the academy principal position between two administrators—one to manage the large number of special education students and one to manage the remaining students. This arrangement (compounded by the personalities involved) ultimately led to confusion, blame shifting, and low morale among faculty who felt that no one was really in charge. The real shift occurred when the whole-school principal retired after the second implementation year. She was replaced by a principal recruited from outside the district. This individual was allowed by district leadership to disband the academies and move the school back to a more traditional departmental organization (another negative example of Lesson 4).

In spite of these bleak developments, bright spots continued to shine at some of these schools. In one of the fast-track schools, the Ninth Grade Academy leader and staff worked hard to build a strong program for incoming students. By implementing interdisciplinary teams, a welcoming, student-centered environment, and extra academic supports, this academy raised the ninth-grade promotion rate from just slightly more than 50% to nearly 75% in the first year. These rates were sustained over the following 3 years. In another fast-track school, the Ninth Grade Academy had little effect on promotion in the first year of implementation. In its sec-

FIGURE 6.1. **Changes in Attendance and Chronic Absenteeism in Five Baltimore High Schools, 1994–2000**

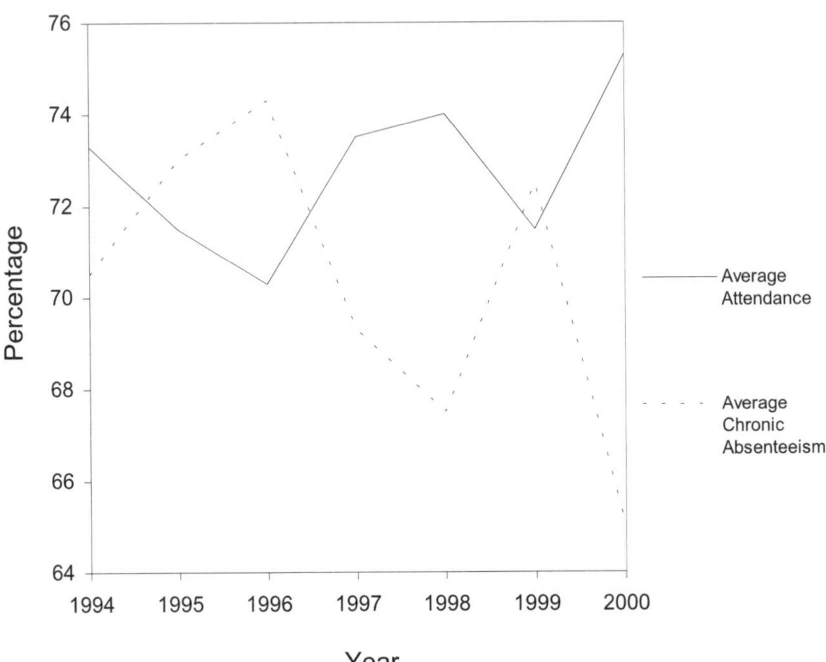

ond year, however, a dynamic academy leader from Patterson transferred to the school to take over the ninth-grade program. His energy, leadership skills, and knowledge of the model helped improve the climate and increase promotion rates from less than 50% to nearly 70% in 2 years. The success of these programs encouraged other high schools in the system to adopt the ninth-grade component and a professional development network facilitated by Hopkins/CRESPAR emerged to support their efforts.

The bright spots of reform described above, and continued efforts at the school and district level to work at and sustain high school improvements have resulted in another bright spot—general upturns on several key indicators. Figures 6.1–6.3 summarize attendance, promotion, dropout, and achievement data available for the five Baltimore schools discussed in this chapter. Figure 6.1 shows small improvements in attendance levels and chronic absenteeism (missing 20 or more days of school) averaged across the five schools from 1993–94 through the 1999–2000 school years. Disaggregated, improvements on each of these indicators were found in

FIGURE 6.2. **Changes in Ninth-Grade Promotion and Schoolwide Dropout Rates in Five Baltimore High Schools, 1994–2000**

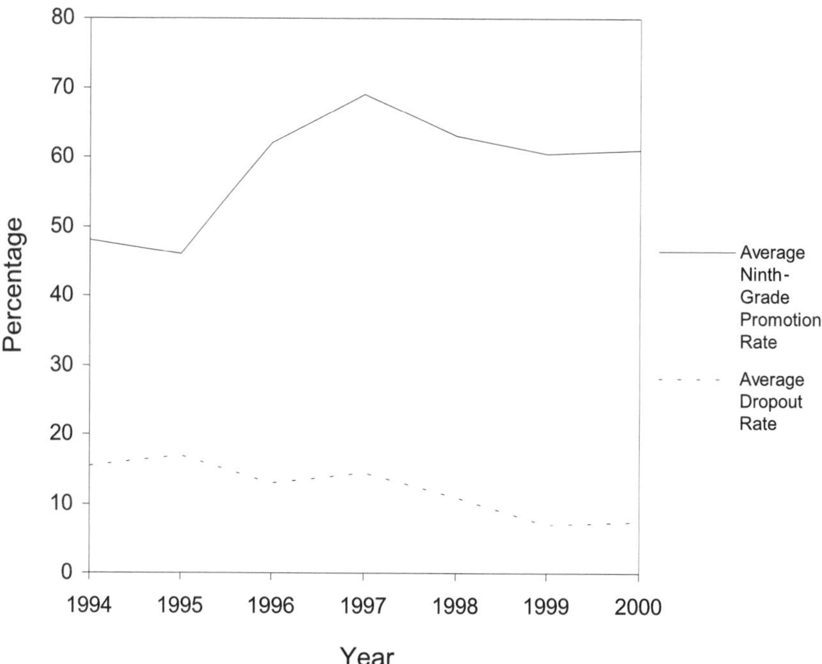

three of the five schools. Because the ninth grade is typically the largest class with the most attendance problems, it is not surprising that the three improving schools included Patterson and the two that developed strong ninth-grade programs.

Figure 6.2 shows more dramatic improvements in ninth-grade promotion rates and schoolwide dropout rates. On average, ninth-grade promotion rates rose nearly 13 percentage points, increasing from 47.8% in 1993–94 to 60.4% in 1999–2000. Dropout rates declined by 50%, decreasing from 16% in 1993–94 to only 8% by the end of the decade. Overall increases in ninth-grade promotion occurred in four of the five schools, and improvements in the dropout rate occurred in all five schools. It should be noted that these improvements in promoting and retaining students in school are likely to interact with attendance rates. Increases in the number of students staying connected to school means that more students who have problems (such as attendance) that would have led them to fail or drop out prior to the reforms are staying in school.

FIGURE 6.3. **Changes in Passing Rates for the Maryland Functional Math and Writing Tests in Five Baltimore High Schools, 1994–2000**

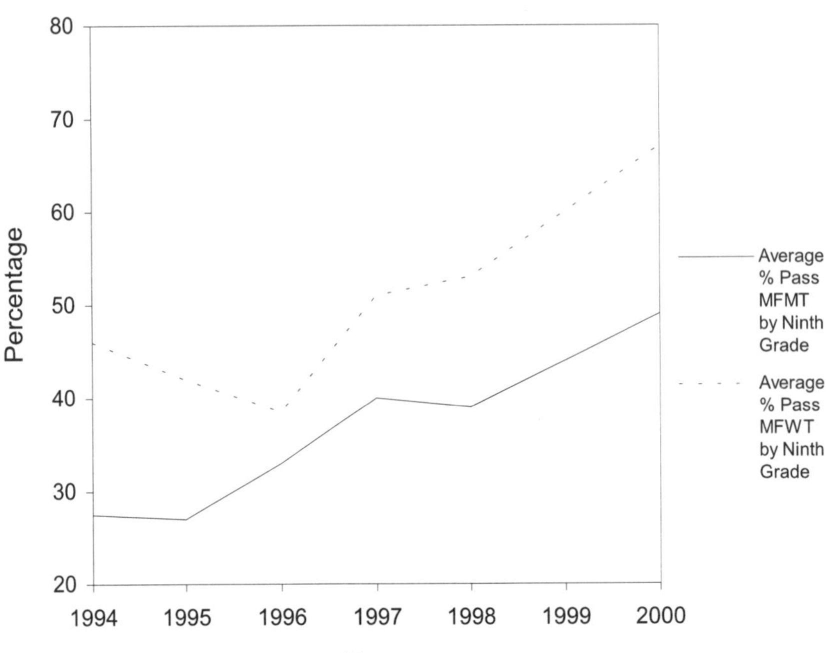

Figure 6.3 shows overall achievement gains across the five schools. While less than a third (28.1%) of ninth graders passed the Maryland Functional Math Test in 1993–94, nearly half passed in 1999–2000. For the Maryland Functional Writing Test, less than half (45.8%) of ninth graders passed in 1993–94 while more than two-thirds (68%) passed by ninth grade in 1999–2000. Improvements on both achievement indicators occurred in all five schools.

These data suggest that, in spite of poor planning, weak implementation in some areas, and reform-threatening leadership changes at both the school and district levels, the combination of state pressure and consequent adoption of Talent Development reforms encouraged improvements in student outcomes in these five schools. School-level indicators are often very sensitive to ninth-grade behaviors because the ninth grade is typically the largest class in the school. Hence, it is not too surprising that the greatest improvement occurred in the schools that implemented strong ninth-grade programs. This speaks to the critical nature of the ninth-grade year. Schools will be well served if they take care in developing their ninth-grade program by selecting strong leaders who understand the student-centered, team-oriented approach and strong, caring teachers willing to go the extra mile to help their students succeed.

CONCLUSION

Pioneers in any endeavor pave the way for those to come, and we learn as much from their struggles and failures as we do from their successes. As shown here and in the previous chapter, the human and technical challenges of whole-school high school reform are considerable. That does not mean, however, that transforming urban high schools for the better is impossible. Early results from Patterson, and sustained results from components of the program at Patterson and other schools, suggest that, even under extremely difficult circumstances, good reform ideas can persist and continue to help students succeed. Moreover, the lessons learned from Patterson and other initial Talent Development sites in Baltimore and Philadelphia have proven invaluable to other schools embarking on a similar reform path. We show how these lessons have been applied and how the reform model has generated further success in the next chapter.

Chapter 7

Lessons Applied: Replicating and Extending the Talent Development High School Model in Philadelphia

Building on the lessons learned during the 1996–97 and 1997–98 school years in Baltimore and Philadelphia, the Talent Development High School (TDHS) model underwent a second phase of development. This phase centered on refining planning-year strategies, increasing the intensity of ongoing implementation support, and developing a Ninth Grade Instructional Program specifically designed to enable underachieving students to overcome poor prior preparation and succeed in standards-based high school courses. These changes brought significant returns to two high schools in Philadelphia that underwent a planning year in 1998–99 and began implementing the model in the 1999–2000 school year. During the first year of implementation in these two schools, improvements in school climate, attendance, and promotion rates were comparable to and, in some cases, greater than those achieved at Patterson. In addition, significant gains in academic achievement were obtained in these schools, as well as in three Baltimore high schools that piloted the Ninth Grade Instructional Program. Both events were extremely important. The first demonstrated that the Patterson gains could be replicated and even surpassed. The second showed that the impact of the TDHS model extended to academic achievement, as measured by the standardized tests commonly employed by school districts across the nation. In the following sections, we elaborate on the process of replicating TDHS in Philadelphia and present qualitative and quantitative evidence of its effects.

A REVISED PLANNING PROCESS

Although the Talent Development High School's initial foray in Philadelphia ran into substantial turbulence at Olney High School, people in the school district, including the principals of several high schools, maintained considerable interest in implementing the model in additional high schools. Based on the experience of prior years in Baltimore and Philadelphia, an improved year-long planning process was initiated in Philadelphia's Edison and Strawberry Mansion High Schools during the 1998–99 school year.

Edison is a large high school of nearly 3,000 students with one of the highest concentrations of Latinos among the school district's 22 neighborhood high schools. It serves a high-poverty population but is housed in a relatively modern facility set off from the immediate neighborhood. Edison has the distinction of having the nation's first career academy. The Electrical Academy was founded in 1969 and is still in operation as a small learning community at Edison (Stern, Dayton, & Raby, 1998).

Strawberry Mansion has a smaller enrollment of about 1,200 students, almost all of which are African American. The school is located in the middle of a high-poverty neighborhood, and nearly all of its students are eligible for free or reduced-price meals. Mansion had a reputation as one of the most troubled schools in the district. It was one of two high schools selected by the district for its school support process and had been a graveyard of multiple prior local and national reform efforts. In 1997–98, the year prior to TDHS planning, Mansion had received unwanted national attention when over 100 police officers were called to quell a lunchroom melee ("News in Brief," 1997).

Implementation of the TDHS model at Edison and Strawberry Mansion evidenced revision to two major and several minor components of the planning process.

Intensive and Sustained Support for Organizational Change

A full-time organizational facilitator was assigned to work half time at each school and provide ongoing technical assistance with the planning and implementation process. In his own words, this facilitator had "lived the model" at Patterson, was knowledgeable of every component, and had experienced the human and technical challenges of implementation. In addition, this facilitator benefitted from a concrete planning year manual that had been developed through the CRESPAR team's efforts to replicate the TDHS model in Baltimore. This manual provided the facilitator and teams at each of the schools with a step-by-step guide and timeline to ensure that each aspect of the model was planned well prior to implementation. Though each school had to adapt the planning process to meet specific needs at their own site, the guide helped everyone involved to be on the same page.

The organizational facilitator provided more intensive, sustained support to Mansion and Edison than any of the previous high schools working with the Talent Development High School program had received. He set up offices in each school and personally facilitated or coordinated facilitation of planning meetings and professional development activities for faculty and staff. He met weekly, and sometimes daily, with the principals. Meetings with the Edison principal regularly began at 7:00 a.m., the only quiet time during the day when they could focus on moving forward the planning process.

The facilitator's close relationships with each principal and other key leaders in the schools were essential to productive planning and implementation. He not only guided the school through the planning process, but also counseled the principals on their budgets, staffing changes, scheduling, and even school politics. Philadelphia high schools presented a unique challenge because they were already organized around small learning communities. Condensing these into fewer, more focused career academies and creating a separate Ninth Grade Academy meant changes in leadership and teaching assignments. The facilitator's knowledge of people in the schools and their positions and relationships to others helped the principals and faculty more effectively negotiate these often painful and contentious aspects of school restructuring. These relationships and the work that resulted from them offered a far more intensive and site-based mode of technical assistance than did the typical summer workshops with school improvement teams or occasional visits supported only by monitoring from afar.

Partnership with Local School Reform Organization

The second major addition to overall planning and implementation in Philadelphia was a strong partnership with a local school reform organization, the Philadelphia Education Fund (PEF). Founded in 1995, PEF is a nonprofit organization that was created through a merger of PATHS/PRISM: the Philadelphia Partnership for Education and the Philadelphia Schools Collaborative. This latter organization had been instrumental in reorganizing Philadelphia's public high schools into "charters," or small learning communities (see Fine, 1994). Through direct programs for students, professional development for teachers and administrators, public engagement, research and policy work, PEF aims to help improve the quality of public education for all children in Philadelphia.

The partnership between the TDHS program and PEF was critical to establishing the model as a priority program at multiple levels of the Philadelphia school system. PEF staff arranged meetings with district and union officials, including the superintendent. They assisted TDHS staff in developing ties with district curriculum coordinators to get new ninth-grade courses approved for Edison and Mansion. PEF also knew the district well enough to recommend strong teachers for curriculum coach positions and facilitated the special assignment of these teachers to the Talent Development initiative. The fund provided political support when TDHS was reviewed by the school board and city council, and helped secure Title I funding. It also provided research staff as well as offices, computers, materials, and payroll assistance for Philadelphia-based Talent Development facilitators. All of these contributions, combined with relatively stable district leadership, helped secure a stronger foothold for Talent Development in Philadelphia outside the individual schools than had been the case in Baltimore.

Changes in Professional Development

More subtle, but no less important, changes to the planning process for Strawberry Mansion and Edison occurred within its on-site professional development and training aspects. The lead organizational facilitator built in to the planning year for the two schools a more systematic approach that included not only attention to the technical aspects of facilities, staffing, and scheduling, but extensive training in the more human aspects as well. He and his co-facilitator involved members of the newly formed academies, and especially the Ninth Grade Academy, in team building and in learning how to lead and work in teams. Teachers participated in training for planning and teaching effectively in extended (80–90 minute) class periods that included the development of lesson plans for specific courses. Perhaps most important, the student-centered philosophy of Talent Development—that all students can learn and that schools must support each individual student in realizing his or her gifts and talents and achieving at high levels—was explicitly articulated and frequently reinforced throughout the planning process in Mansion and Edison. This attention to shifting the ethos in these schools from adult convenience to student success played an important role in the changes that took place in adult and student attitudes about their school the following year.

IMPACT ON SCHOOL CLIMATE AND ATTENDANCE

The more intensive and sustained planning effort paid off in both Mansion and Edison. When the schools opened as Talent Development High Schools in the fall of 1999, there was a palatable sense that dramatic reform was underway. The reorganization of the school into separate academies each with its own teachers, space in the building, and leadership led to instant improvements in school climate that were noticed by students and teachers alike. It quickly became clear that the schools were better positioned to succeed with their core mission of educating and graduating students.

Dick Corbett and Bruce Wilson, two independent researchers hired by the Philadelphia Education Fund to conduct a qualitative evaluation of the TDHS model on student behavior and perspectives, interviewed a total of 148 ninth- and tenth-grade students who attended either Mansion or Edison during the school year. They report that:

> In interview after interview, students shook their heads in amazement at what a difference a year made. Tenth grade students said that the school was better than the year before. Ninth graders (most of whom had attended middle school in the same building) said that the high school was better than what they had seen from their front-row vantage point in the eighth grade and that the entire building had a previously-unfelt calmness and order. They observed, for example, that the stairwells in the five story building had always been a gathering place—for trash, graffiti, and people—and now they were remarkably free of all three. . . . Most telling, students noted was the almost complete lack of fights. To be sure, students still verbally abused one another—both jokingly and sincerely—but somehow, they said, none of this had become physical. (Corbett & Wilson, 2000, p. 7)

The impressions of the students interviewed by Corbett and Wilson are supported by data on student discipline and behavior. Suspensions dropped dramatically at both schools. At Strawberry Mansion they declined from 125 in the 1998–99 school year to 37 during the first implementation year of the TDHS model in 1999–2000. At Edison suspensions fell from 1,049 to 788. Even greater declines were recorded in the number of student arrests, which fell from 62 to 16 at Mansion and from 125 to 21 at Edison. Beyond these declines in measures of the most serious discipline infractions, students and teachers also noted a significant decline in the general disorder characteristic of many large urban schools. Three-quarters of the upper-class students surveyed reported that there were fewer students in the hallway and that school was noticeably cleaner than during the prior year (Philadelphia Education Fund, 2000).

Students and teachers attributed some of the improvements in climate to the physical breakup of each school into smaller schools within the school, and in particular to the creation of a separate Ninth Grade Success Academy. It is clear, however, from student and teacher interviews and survey results, that the driving force behind the improved climate, and the increases in attendance that followed, was the stronger and more positive interaction between students and teachers. Again and again students reported the positive effects of teachers who held firm in their expectations for good behavior, reached out to help them succeed, and had the time to make sure that students understood the material being presented in class. After being asked how his school was different this year, one student who had failed most of his classes the previous year, but who was now getting Bs and Cs said, "They [teachers] know us better and they know if we are supposed to be there. They all care more this year. They won't settle for you failing. . . . The teachers are better" (Corbett & Wilson, 2000, p. 17). Three key pieces of the TDHS model appear to have played a central role in creating a more orderly, supportive, and effective teaching and learning environment.

Teaching Teams

The first piece was the formation of interdisciplinary teams of six teachers who instructed a common group of 180 students in each Ninth Grade Academy. The teams shared a common planning period and were led by a respected colleague who served as team leader with an extra nonteaching period to organize the team process. The teams enabled teachers to work collaboratively to create stronger bonds with, and improve the behaviors of, a manageable number of students. This, in turn, meant that more collective time was spent throughout the school year calling students who where absent and helping to enforce good student behavior, than in prior years when these tasks where delegated to a few overwhelmed individuals.

Students clearly recognized and responded to these efforts. As one student said, "I don't feel like I have to do things myself. I have someone [the ninth-grade team] to help us. You know they [teachers] are there to help you before you go home. They don't let you give excuses. They are there for you, like family" (Corbett & Wilson, 2000, p. 6). Another student stated, "The teachers are more strict. They deal with problems immediately. You can't roam the building anymore. They know our faces. We have ID cards which is good. It is harder to cut. You are going to get caught no matter what" (p. 15).

Overall, significant gains were achieved in two key indicators of student attachment to schooling. Of the students surveyed in the TDHS schools, 83% reported that "most teachers know your name," compared to 65% of students in two matched control schools. Moreover, schoolwide attendance increased from 73% to 77% at Mansion and from 66% to 71% at Edison (Philadelphia Education Fund, 2000).

Focus on Student Success

Another driving force in establishing a stronger teaching and learning climate was a unified message sent by the schools' top administrators that the focus of school was no longer on "keeping the lid on" but on student success. At both schools, principals modeled this behavior by being at the front door to greet students every day, and by relentlessly preaching the importance of collective effort centered around providing students with the structures and supports they needed to succeed. Just as important, each principal reorganized the budget to make the TDHS reform the central focus of the school's spending. Among other things, this enabled each school to open an after-hours Twilight School, as in Baltimore.

Team leaders then took the idea of organizing the school around student success a step further. They worked with their ninth-grade teams to provide students with multiple supports including one-on-one report card counseling (to provide students with strategies for improving their grades), creating smaller classes for the struggling students, and developing individual recovery plans for students failing multiple courses. Guided by the TDHS on-site organizational facilitator, the teams came to view their mission as doing what it takes to get their students to earn promotion to the tenth grade.

Evidence of this new ethos can be found in the programs developed for students who where repeating ninth grade for the second or third time. These programs used a combination of after-school, Saturday school, and summer school along with regular classes to catch students up and allow them to rejoin their peers in the upper grades by mid-year. As one student put it:

> The school said they got tired of having older kids not pass their classes. But I never thought they'd get it together. In September, when I went into the gym to get my roster I saw the ninth and tenth grade lines. I just went to the ninth grade line because with 5 Fs I was pretty sure I was going to be left back. I was reluctant to go to class. But I went and . . . all the classes had one thing in common. They all told us this was our second chance and that we could make up the four credits we needed [to advance to tenth grade in 5 months]. My advisory teacher set us down and told us our chances. The Success Academy coordinator came and told us, too. They said we had two choices: (1) if we passed we would move up to 10th grade; or (2) if not, we would be put in Twilight. That got me to thinking, when they told us we had a chance to make up 10 months in 5. From that day my goal was to get out of ninth grade by February. (Corbett & Wilson, 2000, p. 36)

Extended Periods

The Corbett and Wilson interviews reveal a final key feature of the TDHS design that helps create stronger student-teacher bonds and an improved learning environment. Three-fourths of the students who were interviewed identified extended periods and block scheduling (i.e., four 90-minute instructional periods per day) as a major reason why teachers were able to work more closely with them. This is a very significant finding because block scheduling and extended periods remain a controversial reform. In particular, many teachers argue that students will not be able to tolerate the longer periods and as a result they will become unmanageable. The student interviews conducted at Mansion and Edison overwhelmingly indicate a different reality. A large majority of students interviewed viewed extended periods as absolutely essential to the creation of an effective teaching and learning environment.

Of the 148 students interviewed, 107 said that they preferred 90-minute periods to the traditional 45-minute period. Significantly, not one of the 41 students who said they liked shorter periods better made the case that they learned more under the traditional system. Corbett and Wilson report that six reasons were repeatedly given by students as to why they liked longer periods. They were:

1. Teachers had more time to devote to explanation,
2. Teachers had time to introduce a variety of teaching strategies,
3. Teachers had time to understand students' strengths and weaknesses and tailor their instruction,
4. Students had time to ask questions and clarify their understanding of the material being taught,
5. Students were able to finish their class work,
6. Students were better able to "keep track" of their classes.

One student summed up the additional supports provided by extended periods by saying, "Before I couldn't get much out of it. Now we can get through the book. Before, it was horrible. There wasn't enough time to review the work or ask questions. I have a bad memory. Imagine having to keep track of seven classes" (p. 28).

It is perhaps the most seemingly innocuous of these reasons—that longer periods enabled students to finish their classwork—which in the long run proved to be the most significant. Corbett and Wilson write:

> Students often describe for us a "cycle of failure" in the classroom. In this cycle, students began a lesson, were unable to finish what they were doing in class, and were given the remainder as homework. They did not do the homework, either because of a lack of understanding or a lack of effort. Regardless, they came back the next day unsure of the previous day's content and yet, launched right into new material. The cumulative effect of combining prior confusion with current work was profound befuddlement. [Students reported that longer class periods enabled them to] listen to the teacher, try the work

> themselves (individually and in groups), ask questions, listen to additional explanations, and complete the work—all in the same time slot. (p. 27)

In sum, the teams, a schoolwide focus on student success, and extended periods combined with the physical creation of separate schools-within-a-school enabled teachers and students to create stronger and more positive relationships. This in turn created a climate more conducive to teaching and learning than either school has experienced for many years.

MOVING REFORM INTO THE CLASSROOM: THE TDHS NINTH GRADE INSTRUCTIONAL PROGRAM

In addition to the planning year revisions, the Philadelphia high schools benefited from the development and implementation of the TDHS Ninth Grade Instructional Program. This program combined a new ninth-grade curriculum specifically designed to help students overcome poor prior preparations in mathematics and English with intensive and ongoing implementation support and professional development for teachers. The development of the TDHS Ninth Grade Instructional Program was driven by three factors. The initial impetus was the experience of the second implementation year at Patterson, which brought with it a large influx of students into the tenth grade who had weaker academic and study skills than the upper grade teachers had historically been used to. These were students who in prior years most likely would have dropped out of school altogether. This changed the classroom experience of upper grade teachers and, as discussed in Chapter 5, helped fuel resentment toward the efforts of the Ninth Grade Success Academy. Second, the early development of the TDHS model played out against a background of increasing standards. During the implementation years at Patterson, almost all of the school's instructional energy was directed at getting students to pass basic skills tests in math and writing that had been developed in the early 1980s. However, it soon became apparent, both in Maryland and in other states, that basic skills tests would be replaced by more challenging standards-based tests that ask students to write essays, read difficult grade-level passages, and explain their answers. Finally, TDHS researchers analyzed district data and quantified the huge achievement gap that entering freshmen brought with them into nonselective urban high schools. In Philadelphia, for example, in more than half of the nonselective neighborhood high schools the typical student enters the ninth grade reading and doing math between the fifth- and sixth-grade levels (Neild & Balfanz, 2001). All of these factors made it clear that a strong Ninth Grade Instructional Program specifically designed to close academic gaps and prepare students to succeed with standards-based high school work needed to be developed and successfully implemented in the TDHS schools.

Key Features of Development and Implementation

The TDHS Ninth Grade Instructional Program has several key features. First, the program is built on the premise that poorly prepared students who are performing several years below grade level come to the classroom with substantial capabilities upon which teachers can and should build. This is a different view than that of most traditional remedial classes, where there's an assumption that students need to be taught a subject or skill in either a simplified or watered-down form. Ninth-grade students with weak reading comprehension skills, however, often have strong oral language abilities and significant vocabularies, and these strengths can be brought to bear to improve their reading. We found that in mathematics, different students had different bases of knowledge. Some students had a good understanding of geometric properties but limited skill with rational numbers. Others could manipulate fractions and had a basic understanding of data but knew little about measurement. These findings suggested to us that the often-heard complaint of students in remedial classes that they already know (at least some) of what they are being taught is true in many respects.

The TDHS Ninth Grade Instructional Program thus attempts to move beyond the largely failed attempts of traditional remedial instruction to provide foundational courses that acknowledge, incorporate, and build upon the intellectual strengths of poorly prepared students, while working to fill in and expand the knowledge, skills, and abilities they need to succeed in standards-based high school work. For example, the Transition to Advanced Mathematics class described below begins with a series of problems of the day, which are designed to draw on students' mathematical reasoning abilities and everyday mathematical sense but do not presume strong operational skills. This enables all students in the class to engage in dialogue in which solutions and strategies are discussed, shared, and analyzed. In the Strategic Reading class, oral literacy skills are highlighted and used as a bridge to reading comprehension through read-alouds and word-play activities. These efforts are then mixed in with direct instruction aimed at improving students' symbolic and operational abilities in mathematics and reading comprehension strategies in English.

A second key feature of the TDHS Ninth Grade Instructional Program is that the three courses (Transition to Advanced Mathematics, Strategic Reading, and Freshman Seminar) were created using a 3-year process of piloting in a few classrooms, refining, field testing in several schools and multiple classrooms, and then refining again. All of this development work was conducted in high-poverty, nonselective high schools. This enabled the course developers to observe closely firsthand what did and did not work, and incorporate suggestions from a wide range of teachers into the final materials. It also meant that, over time, the courses were built to meet the often unique challenges found in high-poverty schools and classrooms ranging from a lack of access to basic supplies and copying machines to a high ratio of new, inexperienced, and provisionally certified teachers. Thus, for example, consumable student workbooks were developed for the Transition to Advanced Mathematics and Freshman Seminar courses so that teachers would not have to be constantly photocopying material. Likewise, teacher resource kits that contained all the manipulatives, reference materials, and basic supplies needed for the courses were developed and provided. Daily detailed lesson guides were also developed for each course to provide a solid framework for new and inexperienced teachers, and a foundation upon which experienced teachers could add their own insights and expertise.

A final key feature of the instructional program is that the courses were designed to be inseparable from the multiple tiers of teacher training and professional development support provided with the TDHS model. Intensive introductory training is followed by monthly follow-up workshops that preview upcoming units and address teachers' questions and needs. These monthly sessions also allow teachers within the school (and across schools where more than one school is implementing in a district) to network and share ideas and strategies. Most critically, the ongoing professional development is supported on a weekly basis through in-classroom curriculum coaching and implementation assistance. This support is peer-based and nonevaluatory. It is provided by a teacher-coach who works with no more than two schools and so is able to create and sustain close working relationships with the classroom teacher-implementers. The type of help the coach provides includes co-teaching, modeling, and troubleshooting; customizing lessons to meet the needs of individual classrooms; and making sure that teachers have necessary supplies and materials, such as working overhead projectors. Coaches themselves also receive support and troubleshooting assistance from TDHS instructional facilitators.

Each of these features—curriculum that begins with an assumption of student ability, a thorough development process, and multiple tiers of training and support—has contributed to the successful development and implementation of the TDHS Ninth Grade Instructional Program. The courses and their impact on teachers and students are described further below.

A New First-Semester Curriculum

As outlined in Chapter 2, the TDHS Ninth Grade Instructional Program is built around three courses students take during the first semester—Strategic Reading, Transition to Advanced Mathematics, and Freshman Seminar. Strategic Reading and Transition to Advanced Mathematics are research-based courses designed to help students who enter ninth grade 2 or more years below grade level to catch up in mathematics and reading and prepare students to succeed in standards-based high school courses. Each course is then paired with the English and mathematics course taught to all ninth graders in the school district in the second semester (e.g., English I and Algebra I), providing students with a double dose of math and English instruction (90 minutes a day for the whole year). Freshman Seminar is a course for all entering ninth graders that teaches study skills and social skills along with units on college and career awareness and technology. It is typically paired with a social studies course in the second semester. In addition to these courses, students take one science course and one elective. As a result, students in schools that adopt the TDHS model spend almost all of their class time during the ninth grade in core academic courses. This is a dramatic shift from past practices in which students often spent half or more of their class time in the ninth grade in nonacademic courses.

During the 1999–2000 academic year, the new first semester ninth-grade curriculum was field tested at Edison and Strawberry Mansion and three high schools in Baltimore. Revised versions of the courses were then implemented during the 2000–01 school year. Teacher and student surveys given at the Baltimore high schools and interviews of students and teachers at Edison and Mansion demonstrate that the majority of students and teachers liked the new courses and believed that they achieved their core goal of helping students overcome poor prior preparations for high school work. As shown in Table 7.1, between two-thirds and three-fourths of the students interviewed at the Baltimore high schools piloting the Strategic Reading and Transition to Advanced Mathematics courses believed that the courses were teaching them new concepts and strategies and, because of the course, they read or understood mathematics better. In comparison, students taking more traditional remedial courses in the control schools were more likely to report that they were reviewing what they already knew. Table 7.2 shows that the teachers field testing the Strategic Reading and Transition to Advanced Mathematics classes concurred with their students and stated that their students were learning more than they would be using a more traditional remedial approach.

Evidence of the impact of the Freshman Seminar course can be gleaned

TABLE 7.1. **Student Views on TDHS Strategic Reading and Transition to Advanced Mathematics Courses.**

In this class, did you feel that you were:	*TDHS*	*Control School 1*	*Control School 2*
Learning New Concepts and Strategies in			
Math	69%	59%	50%
Reading	62%	41%	
Reviewing What You Already Know in			
Math	31%	40%	50%
Reading	35%	53%	

Percentage of Students Who Agree	*TDHS*	*Control School 1*	*Control School 2*
Because of this class I read better.	60%	45%	
Because of this class I understand math better.	75%	53%	45%

Note: Reading data for Control School 2 are not reported because while this school gave children a "double dose" of English instruction, the curriculum did not include an alternative reading program as it did in Control School 1 and the TDHS School.

from the Corbett and Wilson (2000) student interviews. Of the 75 ninth graders they interviewed, 55 at Edison and Mansion reported that Freshman Seminar was a positive and useful course. The following comment of one student captures the views expressed by many:

> It helps you with all your other classes. It shows you how to study, how to take notes, how to take your time with your work, and how to pay attention . . . If you had bad study habits, it would help you do better in all your classes. (p. 30)

TABLE 7.2. Teacher Views on TDHS Strategic Reading and Transition to Advanced Mathematics Courses

Did students learn more than they would have using a more traditional remedial approach?	Yes	Somewhat	No
Strategic Reading (N=9)	66%	33%	0%
Transition to Advanced Math (N=10)	60%	40%	0%

Intensive Implementation Support: Curriculum Coaches and Ongoing Professional Development

As we described above, teachers of the three first-semester TDHS ninth-grade courses were provided with multiple tiers of implementation support. All teachers received 2 full days of initial training. In Baltimore, training was followed by monthly workshops that previewed upcoming units and the instructional strategies that they employed. Respected teachers, placed on special assignment from the school district to the TDHS project, were trained as coaches to work directly with teachers in their classrooms, as described previously. Instructional facilitators delivered the initial teacher training, helped design the monthly workshops, gave demonstration lessons, and provided ongoing assistance to the curriculum coaches.

Survey results from the three Baltimore schools piloting the TDHS Ninth Grade Instructional Program in 1999–2000 show that teachers viewed these multiple tiers of implementation support as crucial. The teachers also indicated that it was the combination of the new courses and their materials, along with the implementation support, which enabled them to teach in more active ways and more successfully. Table 7.3 shows that large majorities of the teachers reported an increased ability to use a wide range of teaching strategies that have been shown to increase student engagement and achievement.

Field Test Results

Edison and Mansion, as well as the three Baltimore High Schools field testing the TDHS Ninth Grade Instructional Program during the 1999–2000 school year, were each matched with a demographically similar control school. Ninth-grade students in both the TDHS and control schools were then given the standardized tests in mathematics and English used in each

TABLE 7.3. Impact of TDHS Ninth-Grade Instructional Program on Teacher Use of Pedagogical Approaches.

Compared to other classes you have taught, did the materials and support given better enable you to:	Strategic Reading (N=9)	Transition to Advanced Math (N=10)
Use a more varied set of activities during the extended period?	Yes—89%	Yes—100%
Use cooperative learning strategies?	Yes—78%	Yes—100%
Use group projects?	Yes—67%	Yes—100%
Have students present multiple solutions or methods? (Or use multiple strategies to construct meaning from their texts?)	Yes—89%	Yes—90%
Relate math (or reading) concepts to real-world examples or experience?	Yes—89%	Yes—100%

school district—the Stanford-9 in Philadelphia and the CTBS-5 in Baltimore. In Baltimore, the CTBS was administrated in both February and May. In Philadelphia, the Stanford-9 was given in April. The students' eighth-grade test scores were then obtained from the school districts to enable analysis of achievement gains. Additional standardized test score data was also collected during the first semester of the following year (2000–01). Students enrolled in the Strategic Reading course in three Baltimore and three Philadelphia High Schools (including Edison and Mansion) were given the Gates-MacGinitie reading test in September and then again in January.

In every case, students in the TDHS high schools outperformed the students in the control schools. Even more significantly, with the exception of reading scores in Philadelphia during the first implementation year, students in the TDHS high schools experienced substantial gains in standardized test scores. In many cases, the gains were of such magnitude that they indicate that students made significant progress in closing their academic achievement gaps.

At Edison and Mansion, for example, the median math growth from April of eighth grade to April of ninth grade was 3.5 Normal Curve Equivalents [NCEs] compared to a .2 NCE decline in the control schools. A median gain of 3.5 NCEs indicates that at least half the students at the TDHS schools were catching up with their peers nationally, while the median student at the control was losing ground (Philadelphia Education Fund, 2000).

Regression analysis conducted on the Baltimore data indicates that students in the TDHS schools outperformed students in the control schools in both reading and mathematics achievement and growth. The average student in the TDHS schools gained almost half a year more in mathematics achievement and nearly a full year more in reading achievement. Statistical analysis revealed that these gains were significant and substantial, controlling for the impact of prior achievement, age, gender, special education status, and attendance (Balfanz & Jordan, in press). The design of the Baltimore study also allowed the impact of the new courses to be disaggregated from the impact of doubling instructional time. Students in two of the control schools also received a double dose of math and English instruction. Receiving a double dose of instructional time absent participation in Strategic Reading and Transition to Advanced Mathematics, however, did not have a significant affect on standardized test scores.

The one case, where TDHS students did not appear to have made substantial gains in academic achievement was reading scores in Philadelphia during the first implementation year. Half the students in the TDHS schools demonstrated some improvement in reading ability, but their gains were not sufficient to keep pace with their peers nationally. Neither were those in the control schools, however, and treatment students in the TDHS schools lost less ground than their control counterparts. The median change in reading scores from eight to ninth grade in the TDHS schools was a decline of 4.1 NCEs compared to a 7.1 decline in the control schools. Overall, 33% of the students at the TDHS schools had positive NCE gains compared to 29% at the control schools.

Analysis of the implementation data for the Strategic Reading course at Edison and Mansion reveals several possible explanations why substantial gains in reading ability occurred in the Baltimore schools but not in the Philadelphia schools. First, the Philadelphia teachers were not provided with ongoing professional development. No further workshops were provided after the initial 2-day training in Philadelphia (the schools did not have enough money in their budget to pay the teacher stipends required by the teachers union contract), whereas monthly 2-hour follow-up workshops were given in Baltimore. Second, the curriculum coaches in Philadelphia was not as well trained or supervised as the Baltimore coaches, and had to provide support to three schools, whereas the two Baltimore coaches had caseloads of two schools and one school. Finally, the English

TABLE 7.4. **Results of TDHS Strategic Reading Course, Fall 2000–01.**

School	*Number who took Pre- and Post-Test*	*Median Initial Reading Level*	*Percentage with Catch-Up Gains (>5 months)*	*Percentage Gaining a Year or More in Reading Ability*
Philadelphia				
TDHS 1	191		58%	47%
TDHS 2	206		46%	34%
TDHS 3	59		53%	29%
Baltimore				
TDHS 1	64	5.6	71%	55%
TDHS 2	231	5.4	44%	28%
TDHS 3	112	5.2	44%	29%

department head at one of the Philadelphia schools refused to implement the course, was overtly unenthusiastic about it in front of other teachers, and covertly encourage teachers to "take the materials, but teach as they wanted."

Further evidence that an initial lack of gains in reading scores in the Philadelphia schools was the result of inadequate teacher support, which in turn led to weak implementation, is found in the results of the Gates-MacGinitie Reading test given to ninth-grade students in September and January of the following school year (2000–01). To improve the level of implementation in Philadelphia schools, a second highly skilled curriculum coach was recruited, enabling each coach to serve only two schools. In addition, monthly follow-up workshops were provided to teachers in addition to the 2-day initial training. Finally, the teacher's guide was revised to provide more detailed guidance. This appears to have paid off. The test results shown in Table 7.4 indicate that almost half of the students in the Philadelphia and Baltimore High Schools had catch-up gains (e.g., they gained more than 5 months in reading ability in one semester) and that a third (and in a few cases almost half of the students) had very large gains—increasing their reading ability by a year or more through a half-year of instruction.

Impact on Course Pass Rates and Promotion to the Tenth Grade

Improved climate and attendance, better instruction, and increased recovery chances led to dramatic improvements in course pass rates and promotion to the tenth grade. The cumulative impacts of the TDHS reforms at Edison and Mansion were large.

At Edison and Mansion, the percentage of first-time freshmen passing English, algebra, and science during the school year rose from 24% during 1998–99 to 56% during 1999–2000, the first year of the TDHS reforms. This compares to a gain from 33 to 39% at the control schools.

Promotion requirements were raised in Philadelphia beginning with the 1999–2000 school year. In prior years, students could be promoted if they earned four credits in any subjects. Beginning with the 1999–2000 school year three of the four credits had to include English, algebra, and science. Even so, ninth-grade students at both Mansion and Edison earned promotion into the tenth grade at much greater rates after the implementation of the TDHS reforms than before. Figure 7.1 shows that, at both schools, the promotion rate (after summer school) rose from the low 40s to the low-to-mid 60s. (Meanwhile, it fell to 30% or less at the control schools.)

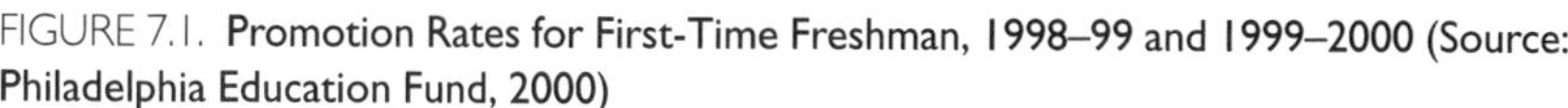
FIGURE 7.1. Promotion Rates for First-Time Freshman, 1998–99 and 1999–2000 (Source: Philadelphia Education Fund, 2000)

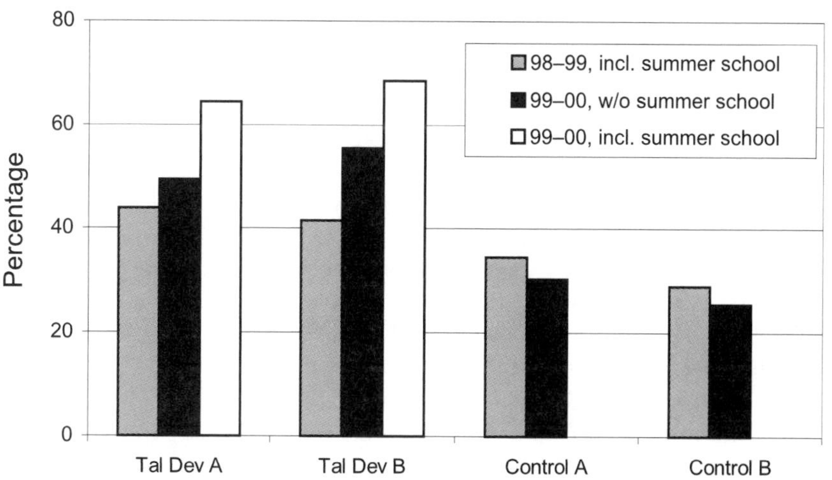

CONCLUSION

The first-year implementation of the TDHS model at Edison and Strawberry Mansion High Schools in Philadelphia was widely perceived by the students, faculty, and school district to be a success. This perception is supported by the substantial data collected by the schools, TDHS researchers, and independent scholars presented in this chapter. A brief survey of the positive outcomes of the TDHS model during its first year of implementation in Philadelphia high schools, however, does not fully convey the complex texture of the year. At both schools, the first implementation year had many successes but also many struggles, and there were a number of obstacles that needed to be overcome. Parts of these struggles and obstacles were the result of incomplete support and attention; others were the result of complex and often unpredictable human reactions to change. A third set of obstacles had their genesis in structural problems that engulf most large urban school districts serving primarily high-poverty populations. All of these underlie the following comments of a team leader at Edison:

> After completing the first year of my tour of duty as a team leader of the Edison Ninth Grade Success Academy, I can only describe the experience as a difficult, tiring, and challenging one. There were many obstacles placed in the way of Edison Team Leaders. . . . All in all the Success Academy Plan is extremely workable if problems concerning staff, and leadership are addressed. (Morrison & Schulz, 2000, p. 91)

The most damaging structural problem was the lack of a stable, fully trained, and experienced teaching corps. Especially at Mansion, many of the ninth-grade students were taught by first-year teachers, apprentice teachers, and long-term substitutes. In the worst cases, students had not one but several of these teachers in the course of the term. The impact of this on students' learning is vividly captured in the following statements made by two students concerning Freshman Seminar:

> We had no teacher. Our first teacher left in October. We had subs until late January when [current teacher] came. I didn't even know what the class was for.

> I didn't get the experience. We had a substitute. The teacher I had left. We just did crossword puzzles. (Corbett & Wilson, 2000, p. 32)

The fact that significant improvements in a wide range of key areas were achieved at both Mansion and Edison, in spite of these problems that plague most inner-city schools, attests to the diligence, perseverance, and ingenuity of the teaching staff and administration at each school. It also suggests a robustness of the TDHS reforms. The implementation of the TDHS model in Philadelphia led to significant gains in school climate, student behavior, attendance, standardized test scores, course pass rates and promotion into tenth grade in two schools that were neither advantaged nor ripe for reform. They succeeded in part because the lessons learned at Patterson and the initial scale-up sites led to further enhancement and additions to both the model and the strategy and processes used to implement it. This, in turn, helped the model have immediate, strong, and positive effects, exceeding even those achieved at Patterson, in some of the toughest schools in a challenging urban school district. This is a tremendously important result because it shows the initial success at Patterson was not solely the result of the individuals who led the effort but stemming instead from the implementation of an interconnected set of reforms that, with care and attention, can be transplanted to other troubled urban high schools to similar strong effect.

CHAPTER 8

Hope for the Future of Comprehensive High School Reform

High schools like the ones described in this book exist in cities across the country. These schools typically promote fewer than half of their 9th graders to the 12th grade 4 years later (Balfanz & Legters, 2001). They are disproportionately attended by poor, minority, and special needs students and show the lowest achievement and highest dropout rates in their districts. Pockets of success may exist in these schools for a few students—a magnet program here, a dropout prevention program there. It is extremely rare, however, to find a large, public nonselective urban high school designed to provide *every* student with the support, motivation, academic coursework, and other educational experiences they need to succeed in further schooling, in work, and in civic life.

As we argued at the beginning of this book, many of the problems faced by urban high schools are characteristic of all large comprehensive high schools, regardless of location. In spite of an official dismantling of distinctions between academic, vocational, and general curricular tracks, these impersonal bureaucratic organizations continue to offer a highly differentiated curriculum that provides a college-bound education only to the most academically motivated and gifted students. If they stay in school at all, students without these advantages take watered-down academic courses and/or vocational classes that do little to prepare them for the workplace. In an era characterized by rapid changes in technology and the emergence of a global economy and society, secondary and even postsecondary education is not just an advantage; it is a necessity. Public high schools must be restructured to promote success for all students, not just a select few.

Few would argue with the claim that secondary schooling for adolescents, especially those living in our large, urban centers, must be improved. The debate of the 1980s and 1990s does not revolve around whether improvement should occur, but rather around what improvement should look like and how it should take place. Two historical studies of the comprehensive public high school published in the 1990s propose contrasting directions for change that broadly describe the parameters of debates in education about the future of American high schools. In the following section, we outline these parameters and argue that current debates, and accompanying efforts to put ideas for change into practice, have led to a pessimism around high school restructuring that threatens the possibility of committed action.

PERSPECTIVES ON THE FUTURE OF AMERICAN HIGH SCHOOLS

In *The Once and Future School,* Herbst (1996) presents a historical analysis of American secondary education spanning over 350 years, from the opening of Latin grammar schools in Boston in 1635 to the end of the twentieth century. He finds that since the late nineteenth century, there has been a persistent commitment to democratic ideals underlying the curricular and institutional development in secondary education. High schooling as it emerged through the twentieth century, however, continually failed to live up to these ideals. Rigid tracking and de facto segregation practices perpetuated social and economic inequality, and the custodial mandate of compulsory secondary schooling has restricted educational opportunities for adolescents outside the high school classroom.

To reinvest the spirit of democracy in secondary education, Herbst recommends a virtual dismantling of the comprehensive high school in favor of educational and/or career pathways of each student's choosing. Following Goodlad (1984), Herbst's plan includes lowering the age of compulsory schooling to between 14 and 16 years. Compulsory schooling would focus on basic academic skills, arts, music, physical education, and exposure to careers. When students have demonstrated mastery of this curriculum, they would receive a certificate to "signify a student's successful completion of compulsory schooling and entry into a world of responsible maturity." The certificate then would "require the student to take charge of his or her further education" (p. 210). Exactly what "taking charge" means is sketchy, but appears to involve choosing from and combining a multiplicity of educational opportunities, including academic and vocational coursework in various types of community, junior, and senior colleges and/or apprenticeships, internships, or paid work in business or industry.

While Herbst calls for a near deinstitutionalization of secondary education, his plan conveys the market-oriented spirit of a broader school choice movement that emerged in the 1990s. Charter schools, vouchers, privatization, and even selective magnet programs and various forms of academies all represent efforts by some educators, policymakers, and community members to provide students and parents the opportunity to choose educational alternatives to mainstream public schools. Choice proponents argue that the presence of such alternatives would offer better educational experiences for children (Finn, Manno, & Vanourek, 2001; Hill, 1999; Nathan, 1996). Competition with these alternatives, moreover, would put pressure on public schools either to improve or to close down for lack of clientele.

In another historical study entitled *The Failed Promise of the American High School 1890–1995,* Angus and Mirel (1999) offer detailed analyses of public high school curricula and students' course-taking patterns through the twentieth century. Like Herbst (and Lucas, 1999), these authors argue that curricular differentiation and a custodial (as opposed to educational) mission have come to dominate American high schooling, to the detriment of all but the college-bound. In contrast to Herbst, however, the creation of a more democratic secondary educational system for Angus and Mirel involves a government-driven, standards-based approach to school improvement. In addition to more equalized funding for urban and rural schools, improvements in early learning, and extra-help programs for low achievers, Angus and Mirel call for more rigorous graduation requirements that emphasize academic achievement, national content standards for academic subjects, and a national examination system. Angus and Mirel further call on educators to develop curricula and methods that enable all students, regardless of background or social station, to master challenging coursework.

Herbst's and Angus and Mirel's perspectives are not mutually exclusive on every point, but do present contrasting views of what high school reform should look like. They also are vulnerable to numerous critiques. Critics of choice plans make compelling arguments that market-based reforms create an even larger gap between advantaged and disadvantaged students. Advantaged students have the economic and social capital to gain access into more selective programs or programs that require additional financial resources, while disadvantaged students are more likely to be left behind in failing and under-resourced schools (Smrekar & Goldring, 1999). Serious questions about the viability, accurate assessment, and overall impact of charter schools also have been raised (Sarason, 1998).

The standards-based approach represented by Angus and Mirel is heavy on increasing educational expectations and assessments from the top down. We have argued in this book that true school improvement requires not only incentives to change, but concrete reform plans and technical, political, and financial support. The standards-based reform approach is weak on how school- and district-based educators are supposed to convince disadvantaged and disaffected youth to jump over an even higher bar to graduate from high school when so many already are failing and dropping out. While many states have put standards and assessment systems in place, and have begun identifying failing schools for possible reconstitution, there remains a great deal of uncertainty around exactly how to help these schools improve, especially at the high school level.

There are many reasons to be pessimistic about the possibility of turning around failing urban comprehensive high schools. As we described earlier in this book, much of the reform focus since the 1970s has focused on younger children because many believe that adolescence is too late for effective intervention. Urban public high schools are typically very large, differentiated organizations situated in large, complex, bureaucratic school systems with rules, regulations, and a chain of command that can make mobilization for change extremely difficult. The departmental organization of high schools, the self-image of many high school educators as primarily subject matter specialists, and lock-step scheduling that leaves little time for reflection pose challenges for reform efforts that call on teachers (and their supervisors) to collaborate and place student success over content coverage. School-level and big-city politics that involve the multiple agendas of policymakers, teacher unions, parents, social activists, and city and state agencies can also pose significant barriers to change. Urban high schools themselves have been subject to so much piecemeal reform over the years, to such little effect, that a culture of failure and resistance now undermines change efforts. Finally, the crushing poverty that shapes the students and neighborhoods of numerous inner-city high schools leaves many wondering whether school restructuring can really make any impact at all in the lives of these youngsters. All of these factors have contributed to a substantial amount of burnout and consequent pessimism among educational leaders and other change agents who have attempted the Herculean task of transforming urban high schools.

Neither choice-based nor standards-based approaches to high school reform offer an antidote to this pessimism. Choice-based approaches actually fuel cynicism about the ability of existing high schools ever to provide high-quality education services to all students (Henig, 1994). While fostering some exciting innovation (e.g., the promotion of smaller, more personalized learning environments and curricula more tailored to students' individual needs and interests), movement toward a free market of secondary education options abandons the democratic purpose of public institutions to provide quality services to all citizens, regardless of their background. The "survival of the fittest" assumption that underlies the heady visions of the choice approach risks leaving many students behind and is more likely to exacerbate than improve the inequities of the current system.

Standards-based reforms sound great to many policymakers, educators, and community members concerned with the low performance of American high school students. They can be depressing, however, to school- and district-based teachers, administrators, and professional development providers who have been struggling for years to raise the academic performance and graduation rates of urban adolescents. The weak link so far in implementation of performance standards and assessments has been the lack of support needed to enable educators to prepare the lowest achieving students to master high-level content and pass the tests. This is not to say that raising the bar is the wrong approach, but without the provision of good, research-based ideas for reform, human and financial resources, and sustained support at the building and classroom levels, urban comprehensive high schools will be hard pressed to raise their students' achievement levels.

RE-ENERGIZING THE MOVEMENT FOR URBAN HIGH SCHOOL REFORM

Herbst and Angus and Mirel come to very similar conclusions about the current state of high schooling and the need for reform, yet present quite different views of appropriate paths to change. Indeed, similar to 100 years ago, we are in a historical moment when we need to make a choice about how best to educate young people in a changing world, and the options are myriad. In this book, we have shared our story of working with large, nonselective, urban, comprehensive high schools to develop, refine, and replicate a model of whole-school reform. Our aim has been to show how, when taken together, the organizational, curricular, instructional, professional development, and technical assistance components of the Talent Development High School approach offer a viable alternative for troubled urban high schools. The process and outcome data we have presented suggest that dramatic improvements in school climate and culture can be achieved when the restructuring components are carefully planned and implemented. We also have found that, with intensive technical assistance and appropriate curricular materials, reforms can penetrate the instructional core of teaching and learning, enabling teachers to raise the achievement levels of very low-performing students and begin to close the gap between these students and their more advantaged peers. Still in an early phase of development and continually vulnerable to the vagaries of short-sighted educational politics and funding levels, entrenched resistance, and our own blind spots, TDHS is far from foolproof. However, with a great deal of humility and a healthy dose of irrational optimism, we offer our story as a hopeful one.

The late 1990s provided other reasons to be cautiously hopeful about the future of American high schools, and urban high schools in particular. Other programs that provide technical assistance to support high school reform include High Schools That Work and America's Choice School Network, which operate on many of the same principles as Talent Development (National Center for Education and the Economy, 2001; Southern Regional Education Board, 2001). Other glimmers of progress are found in the numerous high schools across the country that have been experimenting with whole-school reform. Many of these schools, including several identified through the federal education department's New American High Schools and New Urban High Schools initiatives, are implementing virtually the same model being implemented at Patterson and other TDHS schools (Hornblower, 1997; Rosenstock; 1998; U.S. Department of Education, 1999). Though still in their beginning stages, TDHS and these other ambitious efforts show promise for realizing a vision of high schools where *all* students pursue a college preparatory curriculum, and are provided with adequate support and a community of caring adults who hold high expectations for their advancement.

Because the final writing of this book took place prior to the passage of a reauthorized Elementary and Secondary Education Act (ESEA), it is yet unclear the extent to which high school reform will be supported at the federal or state levels in the coming years. As we mentioned in Chapter 1, the U.S. federal government under the Clinton administration acknowledged the need for school-based support in 1997 through its Comprehensive School Reform Demonstration (CSRD) program. Other federal grants programs to support completion of comprehensive high school reform designs and increase technical assistance for schools, especially in rural areas, also enabled the scaling-up and broader dissemination of effective practices.

It now appears likely that the CSRD program will be continued under the Bush administration. The Bush administration's education agenda, "No Child Left Behind," also proposes additional funds to needy schools and districts, and to lower to 40% the poverty threshold that schools would need to demonstrate to use Title I funds for schoolwide reform. Though legislation passed in 1999 providing $45 million for the development of smaller schools or smaller learning communities in public high schools (P.L. 106-113) is in jeopardy, it is hoped that funds will be made available to the states to continue supporting the high schools awarded the initial planning grants.

In general, improving high schools, urban or otherwise, does not stand out as a major priority for the Bush administration. Proposed literacy funding is geared toward young children, special impact aid is targeted elsewhere, and proposed national annual assessments stop at the eighth grade.

We have some concerns that the emphasis on state-level standards and assessments combined with the administration's desire to increase choice programs may undermine reform in urban high schools. Low-performing urban high schools are least likely to perform well in a standards and assessment program and hence are most vulnerable to sanctions and closure, and to losing motivated teachers, administrators, and students to the lure of choice-based alternatives. Lacking a crystal ball, however, we can only remain hopeful that states will attack the achievement gap by taking on the challenge of improving urban high schools. In any case, the details of this ESEA reauthorization and subsequent implementation will likely play a large role in the future of urban education.

In addition to federal and state programs, private philanthropies such as the Gates Foundation, the Carnegie Foundation, and Soros's Open Society Institute have begun major initiatives to support comprehensive school- and district-level reform. In contrast to the federal government, high schools appear near the top of the agenda in these initiatives. While it is too soon to tell whether these programs will stimulate and support successful reform in urban high schools for all students, their presence suggests the possibility of positive change.

Finally, one of the most hopeful signs for whole-school high school reform in urban areas and across the nation is that critiques of the comprehensive high school are now being translated into concrete ideas and practical reform strategies. Moreover, restructuring high schools appear to be converging on many of the same ideas and strategies. The American Youth Policy Forum's (2000) report *High Schools of the Millennium* offers lists of principles and characteristics from 11 different sources (primarily programs) designed to support high school reform efforts. The overlap of ideas and strategies among these programs, and among others not listed, is striking. In the old days, so many people and organizations calling for the same kind of change used to be called a movement. We believe that a movement has begun and that momentum is building toward the birth of new and improved American high schools that serve all students well.

RECOGNIZING THE REALITIES OF REFORM

While there are grounds for hope, this book also aims to communicate that transforming high schools, and especially urban high schools, to serve all students well is no mean task. We conclude this book with a discussion of issues gleaned from our experience that educators, policymakers, and reformers external to the school system must grapple with as part of the process of whole-school high school reform.

It's Not Easy

High school reform efforts in the late 1980s and early 1990s, most notably the Coalition of Essential Schools and the Philadelphia Education Collaborative, resonate with our own experience of the difficult, labor-intensive, frustrating, exhausting, and exhilarating work involved in transforming high schools (Fine, 1994; Muncey & McQuillan, 1996). The foregoing chapters point to numerous barriers to implementing Talent Development High School reforms in large, urban high schools. Aspects of this work that stand out as especially challenging include the following.

Balancing a Reform Blueprint with Necessary Local Adaptation. In the early 1990s, school restructuring was an amorphous concept. Concepts drawn from change efforts in business and industry and emerging constructivist perspectives on teaching and learning offered some guidance (Cohen & Lotan, 1997; Pallas & Neumann, 1995). School restructuring's most concrete manifestation, however, was found in devolving decision-making authority to the district and school levels. The reigning belief was that if teachers and administrators were just given the latitude, they would create the organizational structures, curricula, and instructional techniques that would generate the most success for their students. It is difficult to know whether this belief has ever really been tested; research shows that even schools that called themselves decentralized in fact remained centrally controlled in many aspects, especially around instructional matters (Bimber, 1994). However, in his review of large-scale studies of educational innovation, Nunnery (1998) finds that "meaningful change seems to be achieved only rarely when the onus of development is placed on schools" (p. 285). This makes sense when one considers that the days (and nights) of school-based administrators and faculty are filled with running schools and teaching students. Ideas or guiding principles for radical change take the back burner to more immediate and pressing demands, making it very difficult even to think outside the box, much less take action to restructure fundamental features of the entire school.

Given this, it is not surprising that increasing numbers of schools are turning to externally developed designs to help guide and implement major reforms (Herman, 1999; Stringfield, Ross, & Smith, 1996). External designs range from assistance with planning and assessing locally developed reforms based on a set of guiding principles to more comprehensive reform "blueprints" or "packages" that include tools and technical assistance to support fidelity implementation of a highly specified reform model. The down sides of going with an external design, especially of the more packaged variety, are twofold. Design developers may either be unaware of or unable to overcome local factors (e.g., politics, turnover of critical staff, commitments to preexisting programs) that undermine implementation. More problematic, however, is lack of ownership and subtle rejection of the model by school-based faculty and staff. Reforms that come into a school from the outside are likely to be viewed as unwelcome strangers imposed on the school from the top down by higher authorities (Datnow, 2000).

As we have discovered, whole-school reform at the high school level requires a tremendous amount of human energy and commitment from every part of the school. Reformers must gain deep agreement from teachers, administrators, students, and others whose lives will be affected by the proposed changes. Deep agreement means more than a pro forma vote pushed through by administrators following a single awareness presentation. It means extensive awareness building over a period of several months that provides all stakeholders with an opportunity to digest the scope of the reforms and ask specific questions about the model and the implementation process. Once the school has agreed to adopt the model, further ownership arises as faculty and staff participate fully in the necessary process of tailoring the model to their school site. Unfortunately, individuals and organizations have a tendency to revert back to familiar ways of thinking and doing, especially when under stress—and there are few jobs as stressful as working in large, urban high schools. Necessary local adaptation should not mean watering down or ignoring core aspects of the model. In sum, we posit that combining a concrete blueprint for reform with agreement and implementation processes that commit the human energy needed to make the reforms come to life in each individual school helps ensure a successful and sustained reform effort.

Finding Time for Planning and Ongoing Reflection and Problem Solving. Traditionally organized high schools are not structured to provide the adults who work in them much time to think and plan, neither individually nor (especially) collectively. Arranging for the time needed to build awareness and attain deep agreement for TDHS reforms, to engage in a collective planning process, and to continue troubleshooting can take some very creative scheduling. At Patterson, a half day of release time every week during planning and implementation years provided time for faculty meetings, academy meetings, and on-site professional development sessions. In our view, this was an optimal arrangement. It must be negotiated carefully up front, however, since schools will need to contend with teacher union contracts and legalities around teacher-student contact hours.

Committing to a Common Core Curriculum with High Standards for All Students. When reorganizing a comprehensive high school into multiple career-focused academies, it is important to ensure that all academies, in both perception and reality, provide all students with college preparatory coursework. The forces of academic differentiation run so deep in high schools that tracking may be sustained in subtle ways. For example, one academy may be designed in such a way that it draws the college-bound students while others become "dumping grounds" for less motivated students (Lee, 1999).

When schools are restructuring, they often are loathe to eliminate special programs. Programs for at-risk students typically bring additional funds into the school that would be lost if the program was terminated. Efforts to eliminate programs for accelerated students usually run into a wall of parental protest and pressure to maintain them. In either case, the teaching positions and resources such programs provide to schools can be difficult to live without. Schools may be tempted to preserve those programs by shifting them "whole hog" into one academy or another during reorganization. Though this may be necessary during a transitional period until funding and parental concerns are effectively addressed, schools must be prepared to evaluate, reorganize, and even eliminate programs that compete with the goal of providing high-level academic coursework to all students.

Another challenge schools will face in this area is the development of teaching resources to teach a common core of college preparatory academic classes in each academy. In many urban districts, neighborhood, comprehensive high schools must compete with citywide magnet schools and suburban schools for teachers. Moreover, high school teachers often are not only specialized by subject area but have developed further specialization within their subject, with strengths in teaching algebra or chemistry for example. In failing urban high schools, many teachers have not had experience teaching high-level courses since so few students populate college-preparatory tracks. Breaking up departments of teachers and distributing them to multiple academies throughout the school means that all teachers must be trained and feel confident teaching at various levels within their disciplines. Transitional structures, again, may be necessary, with upper-grade students crossing academies for upper-level courses like physics and calculus until teachers for those courses can be placed in their academies. Schools also are using distance learning and early enrollment in community college courses to place students in advanced courses.

Finally, as we described in Chapter 5, schools and school systems must closely examine how the growing number of special education students will be served in wall-to-wall academy schools. There appears to be a disconcerting level of denial throughout the system about the amount of resources that are actually required to realize the current movement toward full inclusion of special education students in regular education classes. Parental, political, and legal pressures can make it extremely difficult to effect any change to the special education status quo. In nonselective urban high schools where often up to 25% of the student body receives some form of special education services, this problem is especially acute. Ironically, while it is these schools that are most likely to be pressured into adopting some form of whole-school reform, reforms can be undermined by the special-education system, as we have seen.

Committing to Integrated Curriculum and Work-Based Learning. The career academy approach is one of the more systematic ways to establish effective connections between academic and work-based learning (Grubb, 1995b). Challenges to this ideal, however, include state content standards and assessment programs that do not support a curriculum that integrates academic and career foci. The emergence of high-stakes testing in core academic subjects for high schools has increased pressure on districts, schools, and students to perform well on academic subject tests that may determine whether a student receives a high school diploma. While many of these students would likely learn more in a more relevant curriculum, the difficult tasks of creating and implementing integrated curricula are liable to fall by the wayside in favor of purely academic instruction. The concern is not that students learning in an integrated curriculum supplemented by work-based learning opportunities would not succeed on the tests, but that districts and schools will not make the efforts to adopt these innovations unless states place an emphasis on both academic and contextual/work-focused learning.

Another barrier to implementing true career academies is the lack of high school-level interdisciplinary and integrated curricula. The Career Academy Support Network based at UC-Berkeley has collected much of what is commercially available and some of what teachers and academies have produced on their own. Much of the burden, however, still rests on teachers and districts to create these curricula, and time, resources, and training are often lacking. The traditionally isolated and subject-oriented culture of high school teaching is itself a barrier. Subject teachers typically view knowledge in their subject as hierarchically sequential (especially in math and science) and hence difficult to teach properly in the context of an interdisciplinary unit, or questions or projects based in the real world. Finally, the superhuman effort it takes to establish and maintain industry partnerships and coordinate meaningful work-based experiences for students requires more than a single administrator or teacher. Career academies must have enough resources to dedicate well-trained staff to coordinate this aspect of their program.

Among the New Urban High Schools, Rosenstock (1998) finds that the barriers to developing work-based learning opportunities exist primarily on the school side, where schools lack the knowledge and resources to establish and sustain strong partnerships. In Baltimore and Philadelphia, school-to-work initiatives at the district level are facilitating the development of industry advisory boards and provide high school academy staff with the training and facilitation needed to "put the career" in their career academies. With funding for these programs on the wane, however, it is uncertain where such support will come from in the coming years.

Committing to Revitalized Instruction. Structural reforms (schools-within-a-school, interdisciplinary teams, extended periods) are necessary but not sufficient conditions for improvements in teaching and learning. Teaching in a 4 x 4 block schedule with 80- to 90-minute periods enables teachers to use varied instructional techniques, cooperative learning, alternative assessment, technology, project-based learning, and more student-directed, hands-on activities. However, unless teachers are trained in these techniques and in using the longer period effectively, instruction will remain unchanged no matter how many minutes are given for a class period.

Professional development for improved instruction must not be modeled after traditional forms of in-service training, in which isolated teachers learn generalized skills primarily through fragmented, one-shot training workshops that are part of district-level, one-size-fits-all programs. New approaches to professional development emphasize the need for teachers to take an active role in their own growth and offer learning opportunities that are coherent; collaborative; long range; and which are closely linked to immediate classroom contexts, school goals, and real curricula (Corcoran, 1995; Fullan, 2001; Little, 1993; National Commission on Teaching and America's Future, 1996; National Foundation for the Improvement of Education, 1996). The TDHS approach includes workshops, monthly follow-up sessions for troubleshooting and previewing upcoming lessons, and weekly in-class coaching—all linked to specific curricula.

Supporting Leaders. The most common hindrances to implementing and sustaining reform are weak leadership and the turnover of key leaders and staff. We have proposed in this book that whole-school reform requires principals and other leaders to be change facilitators, delegate authority, and yet make the tough decisions when necessary. As we and others have found, principals often feel pressured by heavy workloads and have difficulty finding a balance between micromanaging change and abandoning (or being perceived as abandoning) the change process altogether (Muncey & McQuillan, 1996). On a large scale, establishing a corps of leaders with these qualities will require changes in pre- and in-service training for anyone in a leadership position in schools. Leadership potential also should be sought out in every corner of a school, not just in the administrative ranks. These leaders must work together as a team and be committed to struggling through the difficult political, technical, and human aspects of reform. It is humanly impossible for even a strong principal to lead single-handedly a whole-school reform effort in a large high school.

One of the most important ways of sustaining reform is to ensure that everyone in the school understands and embraces the reforms, and can articulate to themselves and others why they help create a more effective teaching and learning environment. This widespread knowledge and commitment can help sustain the changes in the face of leadership turnover. It is not enough, however. New leaders must be groomed for leadership positions before those positions become vacant, and they must be required to demonstrate during a probationary period full commitment to the reforms in action and in deed. Multiyear contracts are also a way to ensure leadership consistency over time.

Finally, outside partners and district and state officials must support building-level leadership. They must maintain a regular on-site presence; be aware of reform activities; and be prepared to facilitate, guide, troubleshoot, and provide resources when necessary. They must walk a fine line, however, between offering empowering support and disempowering micromanagement, and be vigilantly aware of how their decisions may affect a vulnerable reform effort.

It's Not Fast

Compared to other approaches that may pilot just curricular and instructional changes with only a few teachers in a school, or others that spend a great deal of time working with school-based improvement teams to generate a reform vision and plan from the ground up, the TDHS approach can show improvement in a school relatively quickly. Marked changes in school climate and adult-student interactions can be seen often in the first months of full implementation. Improvements in attendance and promotion also may occur during the first implementation year.

These changes typically presuppose, however, that the school has spent the prior 12–18 months planning. In Chapter 6, we demonstrate why time for planning is so crucial to the successful opening of a Talent Development High School. Schools cannot expect to completely reorganize overnight, or even over a summer. Schools must take time to build awareness about the TDHS approach and achieve deep agreement among stakeholders to adopt the model. District support and adequate funding for further planning and implementation also must be negotiated at this point.

We recommend the awareness-building process take place in the spring prior to the planning year.

Once the school has agreed to adopt the model, proposals for academy ideas may be solicited and developed during the summer or the first month of the planning year. The remainder of the planning year is spent on academy formation, academy selection by teachers, academy selection by students, start-up training for ninth-grade courses and teaching in the extended period, course pathway development, facilities changes, and staffing and scheduling. All along the way, committees and teams are using their creativity and making collective decisions about how the reforms will be implemented in their school. In our experience with TDHS, we have found that participation in this early work of whole-school reform is not only essential to its success, but is also an important process through which faculty and staff become more deeply invested in and enthusiastic about the overall effort. While it may be possible to make a school look different without this energy, commitment, and sense of ownership, it will not feel different, and the change will be a hollow, contrived, short-lived experience.

Other aspects of the model, including instructional improvement and career academy development, may be focused on once implementation is underway, partly because not everything can be accomplished during the planning period, but also because these elements are ongoing processes that require a great deal of time, attention, and creativity. Training teachers to incorporate unfamiliar instructional techniques such as cooperative learning and more active, contextual, thematic, or project-based approaches takes a considerable amount of time. Teachers must not only learn the techniques, but also practice them over and over with in-class coaching and peer support. This moves more quickly when the curriculum is written for such approaches, as is the case with the TDHS ninth-grade transition courses. Very little curricula exist, however, to support career academy teachers in using these techniques. The Career Academy Support Network based in Berkeley, California now serves as a clearinghouse for courses that integrate career themes into academic courses. Much of the burden, however, still remains on teachers to adapt or create new courses.

Even under the best of circumstances, building a full-fledged career academy that provides not only career-themed academic and elective courses, but also provides work-based learning opportunities for students can take years. Funding and training for full-time coordinators must be found, industry advisory boards established, work-based experiences must be set up and students prepared for them, and curricula must be written that link the work-based and school-based experiences. Each of these critical aspects of career academies will take time and resources to establish and sustain.

Finally, simply working out the kinks in facilities changes, ongoing staffing issues, course offerings, and extra help systems requires several years of attention and effort. Three to 5 years has been the general time period in which reform initiatives have been expected to prove their mettle, and we would expect improvements in all areas to be apparent in TDHS schools within that time frame. However, we also have come to expect that external facilitation in a school implementing TDHS reforms may need to be sustained indefinitely, or at least until there is sufficient cultural change and support capacity at the school and district levels to ensure continuation of the model. Reform, moreover, is not so much a state to be achieved as a cycle of reflection and action in which healthy organizations are continuously engaged.

It's Not Cheap

We have argued in previous sections that whole-school, high school reform demands more than inspiring presentations, facilitated goal-setting, and occasional follow-up visits. Instead, successful whole-school, high school change requires continual on-site presence of organizational and instructional facilitators, concrete manuals and curricular materials, and regular assessment and feedback. It also requires teacher release time for ongoing planning, major changes to school facilities (which often include basic repairs and improvements to dilapidated buildings), and additional staffing in core subject areas and in leadership roles.

All of this requires a substantial financial investment. The current estimate of funding needed to support a TDHS planning year is about $150,000, which covers organizational facilitation, materials, start-up training, baseline data collection, and a small budget for facilities changes (signs, walls, phones in each academy, etc.). The first 3 implementation years cost about $300,000 per year for both on-site organizational and instructional training and facilitation, curricular materials, remote and on-site technical assistance from TDHS design team members, operating expenses for principal and academy/team leader meetings, professional development for leaders and faculty, and further facilities changes. Costs of release time for planning, additional staff (estimated at 11% with the block schedule), Twilight School, and other improvements (e.g., computer and science labs) are not included in this figure and will vary depending on the size and condition of the school.

A frequently unanticipated cost of success in a TDHS school is the funding needed to support the additional students who are promoted and stay in school. We have found that budgets for large, comprehensive high schools often are based on an assumption of failure. School budgets are determined by a formula averaging previous years' enrollments. In our experience, a high school that succeeds in reducing its dropout rate and promoting a significantly larger number of students must fight to convince the central office to provide additional staff to meet the increased enrollment. This experience raises important questions. Are we able and willing to pay the price of providing a quality secondary education for all our nation's youth, and our inner-city youth in particular?

CONCLUSION

Additional challenges to those discussed above are certain to be identified as high schools continue their efforts and as more high schools adopt the reforms. There is no doubt that restructuring comprehensive high schools is a very difficult task that requires tremendous coordination of effort and resources. The current context of standards-based reform, high-stakes testing, and debates around school choice make it even more challenging. Just because it is hard does not mean that it should not be attempted, however. A recent study suggests that there are between 200 and 300 large, comprehensive high schools in the nation's 35 largest cities that promote fewer than 50% of their students from 9th to 12th grade in 4 years (Balfanz & Legters, 2001). This would seem a manageable number and a place to start a committed restructuring effort.

Whole-school reform is finally taking center stage in the education arena. More and more educators understand that piecemeal reform too often produces a confusing and inefficient proliferation of programs that generate resource battles, reinforce inequity, and ultimately help only a few students. Nowhere is this more apparent than in large, urban comprehensive high schools where a complex, differentiated, and often highly politicized organizational structure has encouraged a bandaid approach to the growing social and academic challenges these schools face. Though headway has been made at the elementary and middle grade levels (Legters & McDill, 1994; Slavin & Fashola, 1998), most inner-city high schools remain in need of sustained comprehensive reform.

In this book, we have described a reform model that offers a viable alternative to the traditional comprehensive high school. The organizational, curricular, and instructional reforms that make up a Talent Development High School are designed to personalize the learning environment, provide extra help to students who need it, build a base for success by easing the transition for incoming students, and help upper-level students prepare for college and careers by linking school work with the world of work.

On the eve of ratifying the largest budget for education spending in our history, the president and U.S. Congress are responding to a loud cry for improved schools. We face an important choice about the kind of secondary education these funds will make possible. Our nation, and especially our inner cities, can ill afford the social and economic consequences of maintaining the status quo. Which direction will we choose?

References

Alexander, W. M., & George, P. S. (1981). *The exemplary middle school.* New York: Holt, Rinehart, and Winston.

American Youth Policy Forum. (2000, August). *High schools of the millennium.* Washington, DC: Author.

Angus, D. L., & Mirel, J. E. (1999). *The failed promise of the American high school, 1890–1995.* New York: Teachers College Press.

Arhar, J. M. (1992). Interdisciplinary teaming and the social bonding of middle level students. In J. L. Irvin (Ed.), *Transforming middle level education: Perspectives and possibilities* (pp. 139–161). Boston: Allyn and Bacon.

Ashby, D., & Ducett, W. (1995, December; 1996, January). Building interdisciplinary teams: Ten things you should know before beginning. *High School Magazine, 3*(2), 12–18.

Ayers, W., Klonsky, M., & Lyon, G. (Eds.). (2000). *A simple justice: The challenge of small schools.* New York: Teachers College Press.

Balfanz, R., & Jordan, W. (in press). *Catching up: Impact of the talent development high schools ninth grade instructional program.* Baltimore, MD: Johns Hopkins University/Howard University, Center for Research on the Education of Students Placed At Risk.

Balfanz, R., & Legters, N. (2001, January). *How many failing high schools are there? Where are they located? Who attends them?* Paper prepared for the Harvard Civil Rights Project and Achieve, Inc. Forum on Dropouts in America, Boston.

Baltimore City Public School System. (1995). *Maryland school performance program report, 1995.* Baltimore, MD: Author.

Baltimore City Public School System. (1997). *Maryland school performance program report, 1997.* Baltimore, MD: Author.

Barr, R., & Parrett W., (1995). *Hope at last for at risk youth.* Boston: Allyn and Bacon.

Barro, S., & Kolstad, A. (1987). *Who drops out of high school? Findings from high school and beyond* (Report No. CS87–397c). Washington, DC: U.S. Department of Education, National Center for Education Statistics.

Bevevino, M. M., Snodgrass, D. M., Adams, K. M., & Dengel, J. A. (1999). *An educator's guide to block scheduling: Decision making, curriculum design, and lesson planning strategies.* Boston: Allyn and Bacon.

Beyers, D. (1997, January 31). For freshmen, a false start: Perils of ninth grade prompt freshmen to try new approaches. *Washington Post,* pp. A1, A10.

Bimber, B. (1994). *The decentralization mirage: Comparing decisionmaking arrangements in four high schools.* Santa Monica, CA: RAND.

Bishop, J. H. (1989). Why the apathy in American high schools? *Educational Researcher, 18*(1), 6–10.

Bodilly, S. J. (1998). *Lessons from new American schools' scale-up phase: Prospects for brining designs to multiple schools.* Washington, DC: RAND.

Bodilly, S. J., & Berends, M. (1999). Necessary district support for comprehensive school reform. In G. Orfield & E. Debray (Eds.), *Hard work for good schools: Facts not fads in title I reform* (pp. 111–119). Boston: Harvard University, Civil Rights Project.

Boyer, E. L. (1983). *High school: A report on secondary education in America.* The Carnegie Foundation for the Advancement of Teaching. New York: Harper and Row.

Boykin, A. W. (1994). Harvesting talent and culture: African American children and educational reform. In R. Rossi (Ed.), *Schools and students at risk: Context and framework for positive change* (pp. 116–138). New York: Teachers College Press.

Boykin, A. W., & Bailey, C. T. (2000). *The role of cultural factors in school relevant cognitive functioning: Synthesis of findings on cultural contexts, cultural orientations, and individual differences* (Report No. 42). Baltimore: Johns Hopkins University/ Howard University, Center for Research on the Education of Students Placed At Risk.

Braddock, J. H. II (1990). *Tracking: Implications for student race-ethnic subgroups* (Report No. 2). Baltimore: Johns Hopkins University, Center for Research on Effective Schooling for Disadvantaged Students.

Bryk, A. S. (1999). Policy lessons from Chicago's experience with decentralization. In D. Ravitch (Ed.), *Brookings Papers on Education Policy, 1999* (pp. 67–99). Washington, DC: The Brookings Institution.

Bryk, A. S., & Driscoll, M. E. (1988). *The high school as community: Contextual influences and consequences for students and teachers.* Madison: University of Wisconsin-Madison, National Center on Effective Secondary Schools.

Bryk, A. S., Kerbow, D., & Rollow, S. (1997). Chicago school reform. In D. Ravitch & J. P. Viteritti (Eds.), *New schools for a new century: The redesign of urban education.* New Haven: Yale University Press.

Bryk, A. S., Lee, V. E., & Holland, P. B. (1993). *Catholic schools and the common good.* Cambridge: Harvard University Press.

Bryk, A. S., Lee, V. E., & Smith, J. L. (1990). High school organization and its effects on teachers and students: An interpretive summary of the research. In W. H. Cline & J. F. Witte (Eds.), *Choice and control in American education, vol. 1* (pp. 135–226). New York: Falmer Press.

Bryk, A. S., & Thum, Y. M. (1989). The effects of high school organization on dropping out: An exploratory investigation. *American Educational Research Journal, 26*(3), 353–383.

Canady, R. L., & Rettig, M. D. (1995). *Block scheduling: A catalyst for change in high schools.* Princeton, NJ: Eye On Education.

Carnegie Forum on Education and the Economy. Task Force on Teaching as a Profession (1986). *A nation prepared: Teachers for the 21st century.* New York: Carnegie Corporation of New York.

Carnegie Task Force on Education of Young Adolescents (1989). *Turning points:*

Preparing American youth for the 21st century. New York: Carnegie Council on Adolescent Development, Carnegie Corporation.

Center for Immigration Studies (1998). *The labor market impact of immigration.* Washington, DC: Author.

Cohen, E. G., & Lotan, R. A. (Eds.). (1997). *Working for equity in heterogenous classrooms: Sociological theory in practice.* New York: Teachers College Press.

Coleman, J. S., Campbell, E. Q., Hobson, C. J., McPartland, J., Mood, A. M., Weinfeld, F. D., & York, R. L. (1966). *Equality of educational opportunity.* Washington, DC: Government Printing Office.

Coleman, J. S., Hoffer, T., & Kilgore, S. B. (1982). *High school achievement: Public and private schools compared.* New York: Basic Books.

Conant, J. (1959). *The American high school today.* New York: McGraw-Hill.

Conant, J. B. (1967). *The comprehensive high school: A second report to interested citizens.* New York: McGraw-Hill.

Corbett, H. D., & Wilson, B. L. (2000, October). *Students' perspectives on the ninth grade academy of the talent development high schools in Philadelphia 1999–2000.* Philadelphia: Philadelphia Education Fund.

Corcoran, T. B. (1995, June). *Helping teachers teach well: Transforming professional development.* CPRE Policy Briefs RB-16. New Brunswick, NJ: Consortium for Policy Research in Education.

Council of the Great City Schools (1998). *Signs of progress: Preliminary evidence of urban school comeback.* Washington, DC: Author.

Council of the Great City Schools/ACT Inc. (1998, January). *Charting the right course: A report on urban student achievement and course-taking.* Washington, DC: Author.

Datnow, A. (2000). Power and politics in the adoption of school reform models. *Educational Evaluation and Policy Analysis, 22*(4), 357–374.

Deming, W. E. (1986). *Out of the crisis.* Cambridge: MIT Press.

Eckstrom, R. B., Goertz, M. S., Pollack, J. M., & Rock, D. A. (1987). "Who drops out of high school and why? Findings from a national study." In G. Natriello (Ed.), *School dropout; Patterns and policies* (pp. 52–69). New York: Teachers College Press.

Epstein, J. L. (1991). Effects on student achievement of teachers' practices of parent involvement. In S. Silvern (Ed.), *Advances in reading/language research, vol. 5: Literacy through family, community, and school interaction* (pp. 261–276). Greenwich, CT: JAI Press.

Epstein, J. L. (2001). *School, family, and community partnerships.* Boulder, CO: Westview Press.

Fine, M. (1985, Fall). Dropping out of high school: An inside look. *Social Policy, 16*(2), 43–50.

Fine, M. (1987, February). Silencing in public schools. *Language Arts, 64*(2), 157–174.

Fine, M. (1991). *Framing dropouts: Notes on the politics of an urban public high school.* Albany: State University of New York Press.

Fine, M. (1994). *Chartering urban school reform.* New York: Teachers College Press.

Finn, C. E., Manno, B. V., & Vanourek, G. (2001). *Charter schools in action: Renewing public education.* Princeton: Princeton University Press.

Fordham, S., & Ogbu, J. U. (1986). Black students' school success: Coping with the burden of "acting white." *Urban Review, 18*(3), 176–206.

Fowler, W. J. (1992, April). *What do we know about school size? What should we know?* Paper presented at the Annual Meeting of the American Educational Research Association, San Francisco, CA.

Fullan, M. (2001). *The new meaning of educational change* (3rd ed.). New York: Teachers College Press.

Fullan, M., & Hargreaves, A. (Eds.). (1992). *Teacher development and educational change.* Routledge & Falmer.

Gardner, H. (2000). *Intelligence reframed: Multiple intelligences for the 21st century.* New York: Basic Books.

Gardner, H. (1983). *Frames of mind: The theory of multiple intelligences.* New York: Basic Books.

Goodlad, J. I. (1984). *A place called school: Prospects for the future.* New York: McGraw-Hill.

Grubb, W. N. (1995a). Coherence for all students: High schools with career clusters and majors. In W. N. Grubb (Ed.), *Education through occupations in American high schools* (Vol. 1) (pp. 97–113). New York: Teachers College Press.

Grubb, W. N. (1995b). A continuum of approaches for curriculum integration. In W. N. Grubb (Ed.), *Education through occupations in American high schools* (Vol. 1) (pp. 97–113). New York: Teachers College Press.

Haberman, M. (1996). The pedagogy of poverty versus good teaching. In W. Ayers & P. Ford (Eds.), *City kids, city teachers: Reports from the front row* (pp. 118–130). New York: New Press.

Hale, J. E. (1994). Unbank the fire. *Visions for the education of African American children.* Baltimore: Johns Hopkins University Press.

Hale-Benson, J. (1986). *Black children: Their roots, culture, and learning styles.* Baltimore: Johns Hopkins University Press.

Hammack, F. M. (2000). *Current prospects for the comprehensive high school.* Background paper prepared for the New York University Seminar on the Future of the Comprehensive High School, Department of Humanities and Social Sciences in the Professions.

Hargreaves, A. (1994). *Changing teachers, changing times: Teacher's work and culture in the postmodern age.* New York: Teachers College Press.

Henig, J. R. (1994). *Rethinking school choice: Limits of the market metaphor.* Princeton: Princeton University Press.

Herbst, J. (1996). *The once and future school: Three hundred and fifty years of American secondary education.* New York: Routledge.

Herman, R. S. (1999). *An educators guide to schoolwide reform.* Arlington, VA: Educational Research Service.

Hess, F. M. (1999). *Spinning wheels: The politics of urban school reform.* Washington, DC: Brookings Institution Press.

Hill, P. T. (1999). Supplying effective public schools in big cities. In D. Ravitch (Ed.), *Brookings papers on education policy* (pp. 419–462). Washington, DC: Brookings Institution Press.

Hornblower, M. (1997, October 27). Rio Rancho, NM: Pointing the way toward a practical future. *Time,* 84–85.

Hornbeck's fix for two ailing schools: New faculties. (1997, February 14). *The Philadelphia Inquirer,* p. 57.

Hottenstein, D. S. (1998). *Intensive scheduling: Restructuring America's secondary schools through time management.* Thousand Oaks, CA: Corwin Press.

Jeter, M. (1998, February 13). Integrated magnet school leaves students poles apart. *The Washington Post,* pp. A1, A12.

Kemple, J. (1997). *Career academies: Communities of support for students and teachers.* New York: Manpower Demonstration Research Corporation.

Klonsky, M. (1995). *Small schools: The numbers tell a story.* Chicago: Illinois University College of Education, The Small Schools Workshop.

Kretovics, J., & Nussel, E. (1994). *Transforming urban education.* Boston: Allyn and Bacon.

Ladson-Billings, G. (1994). *The dreamkeepers: Successful teachers of African American children.* San Francisco: Jossey-Bass.

Langland, C. (1997, February 10). Longer classes help learning, school's study finds. *The Philadelphia Inquirer,* p. B2.

LaPoint, V., Jordan, W., McPartland, J. M., & Penn Towns, D. (1996, September). *The Talent Development High School: Essential components* (Report No. 1). Baltimore: Johns Hopkins University/Howard University, Center for Research on the Education of Students Placed At Risk.

Lee, V. E. (1999, April). *Personalism and academic press: Complications of sustaining social capital in six high schools.* Paper presentation at the American Educational Research Association Annual Conference, Montreal, Canada.

Lee, V. E., Bryk, A. S., & Smith, J. B. (1993). The organization of effective secondary schools. In L. Darling-Hammond (Ed.), *Review of Research in Education* (pp. 171–267). Washington, DC: American Educational Research Association.

Lee, V. E., & Eckstrom, R. B. (1987). Student access to guidance counseling in high school. *American Educational Research Journal, 24*(2), 287–310.

Lee, V. E., & Smith, J. B. (1995, October). Effects of high school restructuring and size on early gains in achievement and engagement. *Sociology of Education, 68*(4), 241–270.

Lee, V. E., & Smith, J. B. (1997). High school size: Which works best and for whom? *Educational Evaluation and Policy Analysis, 19*(3), 205–227.

Lee, V. E., & Smith, J. B. (2001). *Restructuring high schools for equity and excellence: What works.* New York: Teachers College Press.

Lee, V. E., Smith, J. B., & Croninger, R. G. (1997). How high school organization influences the equitable distribution of learning in mathematics and science. *Sociology of Education, 70*(2), 128–150.

Legters, N. E. (1996). *Intensification or professionalization: High school restructuring and teachers' work experiences.* Unpublished doctoral dissertation, Johns Hopkins University, Baltimore, MD.

Legters, N. E. (2000). Small learning communities meet school-to-work: Whole-school restructuring for urban comprehensive high schools. In M. G. Sanders

(Ed.), *Schooling students placed at risk* (pp. 309–337). Mahwah, NJ: Lawrence Erlbaum Associates.

Legters, N. E., & Durham, R. (in press). *Six degrees of difficulty: Characteristics of students entering non-selective urban high schools.* Center Report. Baltimore, MD: Johns Hopkins University/Howard University, Center for Research on the Education of Students Placed At Risk.

Legters, N. E. & McDill, E. (1994). Rising to the challenge: Emerging strategies for educating at-risk youth. In R. J. Rossi (Ed.), *Schools and students at risk: Context and framework for positive change* (pp. 23–50). New York: Teachers College Press.

Leithwood, K., Jantzi, D., & Steinbach, R. (1998). Leadership and other conditions which foster organizational learning in schools. In K. Leithwood & K. Seashore Louis (Eds.), *Organizational learning in schools* (pp. 67–90). The Netherlands: Swets & Zeitlinger.

Little, J. W. (1990). The persistence of privacy: Autonomy and initiative in teachers' professional relations. *Teachers College Record, 91*(4), 509–536.

Little, J. W. (1993). Teachers' professional development in a climate of educational reform. *Educational Evaluation and Policy Analysis, 15*(2), 129–151.

Little, J. W. (1995). Subject affiliation in high schools that restructure. In L. S. Siskin & J. W. Little (Eds.), *The subjects in question: Departmental organization and the high school* (pp. 172–200). New York: Teachers College Press.

Little, J. W., & McLaughlin, M. W. (Eds.). (1993). *Teacher's work: Individuals, colleagues, and contexts.* New York: Teachers College Press.

Louis, K., & Miles, M. (1990). *Improving the urban high school: What works and why.* New York: Teachers College Press.

Lucas, S. R. (1999). *Tracking inequality: Stratification and mobility in American high schools.* New York: Teachers College Press.

Mac Iver, D. J., & Epstein, J. L. (1991). Responsive practices in the middle grades: Teacher teams, advisory groups, remedial instruction, and school transition programs. *American Journal of Education, 99*(4), 587–622.

Mac Iver, M., Legters, N. E., & Durham, R. (in press). *What happened to the class of 1998? A cohort analysis of dropout, attainment, and postsecondary enrollment among students attending non-selective urban high schools.* Center Report. Baltimore: Johns Hopkins University/Howard University, Center for Research on the Education of Students Placed At Risk.

Marsh, D. D., & Codding, J. B. (1999). *The new American high school.* Thousand Oakes, CA: Corwin Press.

Maryland State Department of Education. (1997). *1996–1997: The fact book.* Baltimore: Author.

Maryland State Department of Education. (1999). *1998–1999: The fact book.* Baltimore: Author.

Maryland State Department of Education. (2001). On-line: http://www.msde.state.md.us

Mathews, J. (1998). *Class struggle: What's wrong (and right) with America's best public high schools.* New York: Times Books.

McCall, N. (1994). *Makes me wanna holler: A young black man in America.* New York: Vintage Books.

McPartland, J. M. (1990). Staffing decisions in the middle grades: Balancing quality instruction and teacher/student relations. *Phi Delta Kappan, 71,* 465–469.

McPartland, J. M., Balfanz, R., Jordan, W., & Legters, N. (1998). Improving climate and achievement in a troubled urban high school through the talent development model. *Journal on the Education of Students Placed At Risk, 3*(4), 337–361.

McPartland, J. M., Jordan, W., Legters, N., & Balfanz, R. (1997). Finding safety in small numbers. *Educational Leadership, 55,* 14–17.

McPartland, J. M., Legters, N., Jordan, W., & McDill, E. L. (1996). *The talent development high school: Early evidence of impact on school climate, attendance, and student promotion.* (Report No. 2). Baltimore: Johns Hopkins & Howard University Center for Research on the Education of Students Placed At Risk.

McPartland, J. M., & Schneider, B. (1996). Opportunities to learn and student diversity: Prospects and pitfalls of a common core curriculum. *Sociology of Education* [extra issue], pp. 66–81.

Mendel, R. (1997). *The American school-to-career movement: A background paper for policy makers and foundation officers.* Washington, DC: American Youth Policy Forum.

Morrison, W. F., & Schulz, L. (2000, July). *Guidebook for team leaders in the talent development high school.* Baltimore: Johns Hopkins University/Howard University Center for Research on the Education of Students Placed At Risk.

Muncey, D. E., & McQuillan, P. J. (1996). *Reforms & resistance in schools & classrooms.* New Haven: Yale University Press.

Nathan, J. (1996). *Charter schools.* San Francisco: Jossey-Bass.

National Association of Secondary School Principals/Carnegie Foundation (1996). *Breaking ranks: Changing an American institution.* Reston, VA: Author.

National Center for Education and the Economy (2001). On-line: http://www.ncee.org

National Commission on Teaching and America's Future. (1996). *What matters most: Teaching for America's future.* New York: Author.

National Council of Teachers of Mathematics. (1989). *Curriculum and evaluation standards for school mathematics.* Reston, VA: Author.

National Education Commission on Time and Learning. (1994). *Prisoners of time.* Washington, DC: Author.

National Foundation for the Improvement of Education. (1996). *Teachers take charge of their learning.* Washington, DC: Author.

Natriello, G. (Ed.). (1987). *School dropouts: Patterns and policies.* New York: Teachers College Press.

Natriello, G., McDill, E. L., & Pallas, A. M. (1990). *Schooling disadvantaged children: Racing against catastrophe.* New York: Teachers College Press.

Neild, R. (2000). *Special tabulation of the Philadelphia education longitudinal study data.*

Neild, R., & Balfanz, R. (2001). *An extreme degree of difficulty: The educational challenge of the ninth grade in Philadelphia's neighborhood high schools.* Center for Social Organization of Schools, Johns Hopkins University.

Newmann, F. M. (Ed.). (1996). *Authentic achievement: Restructuring schools for intellectual quality.* San Francisco: Jossey-Bass.

Newmann, F. M. (Ed.) (1992). *Student engagement and achievement in American secondary schools.* New York: Teachers College Press.

Newmann, F. M., & Wehlage, G. G. (1995). *Successful school restructuring.* Madison, WI: Center on Organization and Restructuring of Schools.

News in brief: 15 arrested in lunch brawl. (1997, December 3). *Education Week*, p. 20.

Nunnery, J. (1998). Reform ideology and the locus of development problem in educational restructuring. In S. Stringfield & A. Datnow (Eds.), Scaling up school restructuring and improvement designs. *Education and Urban Society, 30*(3), 269–276.

Oakes, J. (1985). *Keeping track: How schools structure inequality.* New Haven: Yale University Press.

Oakes, J., & Lipton, M. (1990). Tracking and ability grouping: A structural barrier to access and achievement. In J. I. Goodlad & P. Keating (Eds.), *Access to knowledge: An agenda for our nation's schools* (pp. 43–58). New York: College Entrance Examination Board.

Olson, L. (1997). *School to work revolution.* Reading, MA: Addison-Wesley.

O'Neil, J. (1995). Finding time to learn. *Educational Leadership, 53*(3), 11–15.

Orfield, G., & Eaton, S. E. (1996). *Dismantling desegregation: The quiet reversal of Brown v. Board of Education.* New York: New Press.

Orr, M. (1999). *Black social capital: The politics of school reform in Baltimore, 1986–1998.* Lawrence University Press of Kansas.

Oxley, D. (1990). *An analysis of house systems in New York City neighborhood high schools.* Philadelphia: Temple University, Center for Research in Human Development and Education.

Oxley, D. (March 1994). Organizing schools into small units: Alternatives to homogeneous grouping. *Phi Delta Kappan, 75*(7), 521–526.

Pallas, A., & Neumann, A. (1995). Lost in translation: Applying total quality management to schools, colleges, and universities. In M. T. Hallinan (Ed.), *Restructuring schools: Promising practices and policies* (pp. 31–55). New York: Plenum Press.

Philadelphia Education Fund (2000, October). *The talent development high school: First-year results of the ninth grade success academy in two Philadelphia schools 1999–2000.* Philadelphia: Author.

Piore, M. J., & Sabel, C. F. (1984). *The second industrial divide: Possibilities for prosperity.* New York: Basic Books.

Powell, A., Farrar, E., & Cohen, D. (1985). *The shopping mall high school.* New York: Houghton Mifflin.

Quality counts '98: The urban challenge—public education in the 50 states. (1998, January 8). *Education Week/Pew Charitable Trust, 17*(17).

Queen, J. A. (2000, November). Block scheduling revisited. *Phi Delta Kappan, 82*(3), 214–222.

Queen, J. A., & Isenhour, K. G. (1998). *The 4 x 4 block schedule.* Princeton, NJ: Eye on Education, Inc.

Resnick, L. B. (1987a). *Education and learning to think.* Washington, DC: National Academy Press.

Resnick, L. B. (1987b). *Instruction and the cultivation of thinking.* In E. De Corte, H. Lodewijks, & R. P. Parmer (Eds.), *Learning and instruction: European research in an international context* (pp. 415–442). Oxford: Leuven University Press/Pergamon Press.

Resnick, L. B., & Wirt, J. G. (1996). *Linking school and work: Roles for standards and assessment.* San Francisco: Jossey-Bass.

Rivkin, S. G. (1994). Residential segregation and school integration. *Sociology of Education, 67*(4), 279–292.

Roderick, M. (1993). *The path to dropping out.* Westport, CT: Auburn House.

Roderick, M., & Camburn, E. (1999). Risk and recovery from course failure in the early years of high school. *American Educational Research Journal, 36,* 303–343.

Roderick, M., Choing, J., & DeCosta, K. (1998). *The student life in high school project: First follow up student outcomes.* Chicago: University of Chicago, School of Social Service Administration.

Rosenstock, L. (1998, April). *Changing the subject: The new urban high school.* Paper presented at the American Educational Research Association Annual Conference, San Diego, CA.

Ruiz-de-Velasco, J., & Fix, M. (2000). *Overlooked and underserved: Immigrant children in U.S. secondary schools.* Washington, DC: Urban Institute Press.

Rury, J. L. (1999). *Educating urban youth: James Conant and the changing context of metropolitan America, 1945–1995.* Paper prepared for the New York University Seminar on the Future of the Comprehensive High School, Department of Humanities and Social Sciences in the Professions.

Rusk, D. (1996). *Baltimore Unbound, A strategy for regional renewal.* Baltimore: Abell Foundation.

Sarason, S. B. (1996). *Revisiting the culture of the school and the problem of change.* New York: Teachers College Press.

Sarason, S. B. (1998). *Charter schools: Another flawed educational reform?* New York: Teachers College Press.

Schorr, L. B. (1997). *Common purpose: Strengthening families and neighborhoods to rebuild America.* New York: Doubleday.

Secretary's Commission on Achieving Necessary Skills (1991). *What work requires of schools: A SCANS report for America 2000.* Washington, DC: U.S. Department of Labor.

Senge, P. M. (1990). *The fifth discipline: The art and practice of the learning organization.* New York: Doubleday.

Senge, P. M. (2000). *Schools that learn.* New York: Doubleday.

Singh, V. P. (1991). The underclass in the United States: Some correlates of economic change. In J. Kretovics & E. Nussel (Eds.), *Transforming urban education* (pp. 57–72). Boston: Allyn and Bacon.

Siskin, L. S., & Little, J. W. (1995). *The subjects in question: Departmental organization and the high school.* New York: Teachers College Press.

Sizer, T. R. (1984). *Horace's compromise: The dilemma of the American high school.* Boston: Houghton Mifflin.

Slavin, R. E. (1986). *Effective classroom programs for students at risk.* Baltimore: Johns Hopkins University, Center for Social Organization of Schools.

Slavin, R. E. (1994). *Cooperative learning: Theory, research and practice.* Boston: Allyn and Bacon.

Slavin, R. E., & Fashola, O. S. (1998). *Show me the evidence!: Proven and promising programs for America's schools.* Thousand Oaks, CA: Corwin.

Smrekar, C., & Goldring, E. (1999). *School choice in urban America: Magnet schools and the pursuit of equity.* New York: Teachers College Press.

Smylie, M. A. (1996). From bureaucratic control to building human capital: The importance of teacher learning in education reform. *Educational Researcher, 25*(9), 9–11.

Southern Regional Education Board (2001). On-line: http://www.sreb.org

Sparks, D., & Hirsch, S. (1997). *A new vision for staff development.* Oxford, OH: National Staff Development Council.

State Agencies Take Hands-On Role in Reform. (1999, June 9). *Education Week, 18*(39).

Stern, D., Finkelstein, N., Stone, J. III, Latting, J., & Dornsife, C. (1995). *School to work: Research on programs in the United States.* Washington, DC: Falmer.

Stern, D. (1997, November). The continuing promise of work-based learning. *Centerfocus,* No. 18. Berkeley, CA: University of California-Berkeley, National Center for Research in Vocational Education.

Stern, D., Dayton, C., & Raby, M. (1998, December). *Career academies and high school reform.* Berkeley, CA: University of California at Berkeley, Career Academy Support Network.

Stern, D., Finkelstein, N., Urpuiola, M., & Cagampang, H. (1997). *School to work: Research on programs in the United States.* Washington, DC: Taylor and Francis.

Stern, D., & Hallinan, M. T. (1997, Winter). The high schools, they are a-changin'. *Center Work (Tenth Anniversary Issue), 8*(4). Berkeley, CA: University of California-Berkeley, National Center for Research in Vocational Education.

Stern, D., Raby, M., & Dayton, C. (1992). *Career academies.* San Francisco: Jossey-Bass.

Stevenson, H. W., & Stigler, J. W. (1992). *The learning gap: Why our schools are failing and what we can learn from Japanese and Chinese education.* Summit Books: New York.

Stringfield, S., & Datnow, A. (1998). Scaling up school restructuring designs in urban schools. *Education and Urban Society, 30* (3), 269–276.

Stringfield, S., Ross, S., & Smith, L. (1996). *Bold plans for school restructuring.* Mahwah, NJ: Erlbaum.

Tyack, D. (1974). *The one best system: A history of American urban education.* Cambridge: Harvard University Press.

Tyack, D., & Hansot, E. (1982). *Managers of virtue: Public school leadership in America, 1820–1980.* New York: Basic Books.

U.S. Bureau of Labor Statistics (2001). On-line: http://stats.bls.gov/ceshome.htm

U.S. Census Bureau (2000). *Summary file 1: Census 2000.* Washington, DC: Author.

U.S. Department of Education, National Center for Educational Statistics (2000). *The condition of education 2000.* (NCES 2000–602). Washington, DC: U.S. Government Printing Office.

U.S. Department of Education, National Center for Educational Statistics (2001). *The condition of education 2001.* (NCES 2001–072). Washington, DC: U.S. Government Printing Office.

U.S. Department of Education, Office of Vocational and Adult Education, New American High Schools Program (1999). *Aiming high: Strategies to promote high standards in high schools*. Washington, DC: Author.

Wells, A. S., & Oakes, J. (1996). Potential pitfalls of systemic reform: Early lessons from research on detracking. *Sociology of Education* [extra issue], pp. 135–143.

Wiggins, G., & McTighe, J. (2000). *Understanding by design*. Upper Saddle River, NJ: Prentice Hall.

Wraga, W. G. (1994). *Democracy's high school: The comprehensive high school and educational reform in the United States*. New York: University Press of America.

Wraga, W. G. (1999). Repudiation, reinvention, and educational reform: The comprehensive high school in historical perspective. *Educational Administration Quarterly, 35*, 292–304.

Yonezawa, S. S. (2000). Unpacking the black box of tracking decisions: Critical tales of families navigating the course placement process. In M. G. Sanders (Ed.), *Schooling students placed at risk: Research, policy, and practice in the education of poor and minority adolescents* (pp. 109–137). Mahwah, NJ: Erlbaum.

Index

Accountability, 3
Adams, K. M., 26
Administrative staff. *See also* Faculty/administrator collaboration
  decentralization of, 52, 56
  top-down administration, 91, 93, 94
African American students
  cognitive performance of, 24
  population increase in urban areas, 44
  poverty of urban, 10
After-school programs, 34, 72–73
Alexander, W. M., 22
American Youth Policy Forum, 140
America's Choice School Network, 139
Amprey, Walter, 48
Angus, D. L., 136–137, 138
Arhar, J. M., 22
Ashby, D., 22
At-risk students, 4–5
  dropout rates and, 20, 22–23
  programs for, 143
  recovery opportunities and support services for, 34
  in transitions. *See* Transitions of students

Bailey, C. T., 24
Balfanz, R., 4, 5, 26–27, 122, 129, 134, 149
Baltimore, Maryland, 43–77, 81–106, 109–113. *See also* Patterson High School (Baltimore)
  achievement gaps among pre-high school students, 11–12
  dropout rates in, 44, 96–97, 98
  impact of economic and demographic change on public schools, 43–45
  magnet schools, 4–5, 48–49
  population decline in, 44
  poverty in, 44–45
  "reconstitution" of failing schools, 45, 46–47, 48, 50, 51, 92–94
  risk factors of high school students, 4–5
  scaling-up in, 101–106, 109–113, 127–128
  state and district responses to school problems, 45–46, 94–96
Baltimore City Public School System (BCPSS), 12, 44, 45–46, 47, 59–60
Barro, S., 20
Berends, M., 100
Bevevino, M. M., 26
Beyers, D., 27
Bimber, B., 141
Bishop, J. H., 23
Blended instruction, 36
Block scheduling, 24–25, 36–37, 55–56, 66, 120–122
Bodilly, S. J., 100
Boyer, E. L., 8–9
Boykin, A. Wade, 24, 29
Braddock, J. H., 20
Breaking Ranks (National Association of Secondary School Principals), 14, 17–18
Brown v. Board of Education, 8
Bryk, A. S., 21, 27, 29, 30
Bush, George W., 139

Campbell, E. Q., 29
Canady, R. L., 25, 55

Cardinal Principles of Secondary Education, 7–8
Career Academies, 23, 32, 33, 35–36
  balancing with whole-school reform, 92
  faculty selection and placement, 52, 55, 104–105
  inter-academy conflicts and, 81–87
  multiple authority figures and, 83–84, 86–87
  at Patterson High School (Baltimore), 51–56, 81–87, 92
  scheduling for, 55–56
  student placement and selection, 52–54
  subject-area department heads in, 57, 86–87
Career Academy Support Network, 144, 147
Carnegie Forum on Education and the Economy, 8–9
Carnegie Foundation, 140
Carnegie Task Force on Education of Young Adolescents, 31
Catholic schools, common core curriculum of, 21
Center for Immigration Studies, 10
Center for Research on the Education of Students Placed at Risk (CRESPAR), 15, 50–51, 58–59, 90, 98–99, 101–102, 104, 105–106, 107, 110, 115
Centralized organization, 29
Central Park East (New York City), 19
Chicago, analysis of 9th-grade repeaters, 5
Choice-based approach, 135–136, 137
Choing, J., 5
Civil rights movement, 8
Classism, 8
Clinton, Bill, 139
Coalition of Essential Schools, 19, 141
Cognition and learning
  of African American students, 24
  in Talent Development High Schools (TDHS), 30–31
Cohen, D., 8–9, 11
Cohen, E. G., 26, 141
Coleman, J. S., 21, 29
Coleman Report, 29
Collegiality
  data collection on, 65
  expectations for change with TDHS approach, 63
Commission on the Reorganization of Secondary Education, 7
Common core curriculum, 20–21, 142–144
Common Purpose (Schorr), 100
Communal organization, 29–30
Community partnerships, 34–35
Comprehensive high schools, 134–150
  achievement gaps among pre-high school students, 11–12
  in Baltimore, 4
  Cardinal Principles of Secondary Education and, 7–8
  common core curriculum in, 20–21, 142–144
  criticisms of, 8–9, 10–14, 18–27, 28
  departmentalization of, 21–22
  diversity and segregation in, 12–13
  enrollment trends, 5
  immigration and, 10, 12–13
  instruction methods in, 25–26
  lack of educational resources, 11
  large size of, 18–19
  outdated character of, 10–14
  perspectives on future of, 135–138
  in Philadelphia, 4
  politics and, 13
  poverty in urban areas and, 10–11, 12–13, 139
  realities of reform in, 140–149
  re-energizing movement for reform of, 138–140
  relevance of schoolwork, 22–24, 144–145
  scheduling in, 24–25

school climate and, 12
segregation and, 12–13, 135
tracking and, 8, 19–21, 135
transitions of students and, 26–27
urban population declines and, 10–11
Comprehensive School Reform Demonstration (CSRD) program, 139
Conant, J. B., 8, 18
Constructivist approach
emergence of, 141
multiple intelligences and, 30–31
nature of, 26
Contextual instruction, 36
Cooperative learning, 26
Corbett, H. D., 118–122, 125–126, 132
Corcoran, T. B., 145
Council of the Great City Schools, 21
Craft model of production, 7
Credit school, 34
Croninger, R. G., 21

Datnow, A., 6, 100, 142
Dayton, C., 23, 115
DeCosta, K., 5
Deming, W. E., 29
Dengel, J. A., 26
Departmentalization, 21–22
Detention after school, 69
Diversity
in comprehensive high schools, 12–13
in Talent Development High Schools (TDHS), 37–38
Dornsife, C., 23
Driscoll, M. E., 29
Dropout rates
in Baltimore, Maryland, 44, 96–97, 98
in comprehensive high schools, 18
data collection on, 111
effects of educational reform on, 111
in School Performance Index, 97
tracking and, 20, 22–23

Ducett, W., 22
Durham, R. E., 12, 13, 97

Eaton, S. E., 12
Eckstrom, R. B., 20, 27
Edison High School (Philadelphia), 15–16
implementation process, 115–122, 132–133
planning process for, 115
Educational reform
effects of high school, 65–77
nature of, in high schools, 3–4
pressure for, 3
responses to criticisms of comprehensive high schools, 18–27, 28
Education Alternatives, Inc., 48
Effects of high school reform, 65–77
on attendance, 70–71, 110–111
on faculty/staff collaboration, 75–77
general observations, 66–67
on school climate, 67–70
on School Performance Index, 73–75, 97
on student achievement, 73, 112
on student promotion, 71–73, 88–89, 111, 120, 131
Elementary and Secondary Education Act (ESEA), 139
Enterprise school system, 46
Epstein, J. L., 22, 34–35

Factory model of schooling, 24
Faculty/administrator collaboration
data collection on, 65
effects of educational reform on, 75–77
expectations for change with TDHS approach, 63
inter-academy conflicts, 81–87
whole-school principal role, 84–86, 92–94
Faculty selection and placement, 52, 55, 104–105

Failed Promise of the American High School 1890–1995, The (Angus and Mirel), 136
Family partnerships, 34–35
Farrar, E., 8–9, 11
Fashola, O. S., 149
Feminist movement, 8
Financial issues, 90, 95, 116–117, 118, 140, 148–149
Fine, M., 19, 27, 116, 141
Finkelstein, N., 23
Finn, C. E., 136
Fix, M., 12
Flexible scheduling, 84
Flexible specialization, in secondary schools, 7
Flex School, 56
Fordham, S., 19
Fowler, W. J., 18
Freshman Seminar, 33, 39
Fullan, M., 31, 38, 145
Full-inclusion model, 89, 96, 143–144

Gardner, H., 30
Gates Foundation, 140
George, P. S., 22
Goertz, M. S., 27
Goldring, E., 136
Goodlad, J. I., 8–9, 20, 135
Grubb, W. N., 23, 144

Haberman, M., 22–23
Hale, J. E., 24
Hale-Benson, J., 24
Hammack, F. M., 10
Hansot, E., 7
Hargreaves, A., 31, 82
Harlem Middle Park School (Baltimore), 48–49
Henig, J. R., 137
Herbst, Jurgen, 3, 7, 135–136, 138
Herman, R. S., 6, 141
Hess, F. M., 13
High Schools of the Millennium (American Youth Policy Forum), 140
High Schools That Work, 139
Hill, P. T., 136
Hirsch, S., 31
Hobson, C. J., 29
Hoffer, T., 21
Holland, P. B., 21
Hornblower, M., 139

ID badges/cards, in Career Academies, 66, 69, 119
Immigration, impact on comprehensive high schools, 10, 12–13
Individual education plans (IEPs), 89, 96
Instructional facilitators, 39
Interdisciplinary instruction, 22, 32, 36, 119
Isenhour, K. G., 25

Jantzi, D., 30
Jeter, M., 17
Johns Hopkins University, 6
  Center for Research on the Education of Students Placed At Risk (CRESPAR), 15, 50–51, 58–59, 90, 98–99, 101–102, 104, 105–106, 107, 110, 115
  Center for Social Organization of Schools, 50–51
Jordan, W., 22, 27, 129

Kemple, J., 23
Keystone provision, 106–107
Kilgore, S. B., 21
Klonsky, M., 19
Kolstad, A., 20
Kretovics, J., 13–14

Ladson-Billings, G., 24
Language experiments, 24
LaPoint, V., 22
Lateness, 69

Latting, J., 23
Leadership. *See also* Principals
  at district level, 45–46, 94–96
  importance of supporting leaders, 145–146
  polarized, 90–92
  at state level, 45–46, 94–96
Lee, V. E., 18, 20, 21, 22, 30, 143
Legters, N. E., 5, 12, 13, 27, 97, 134, 149
Leithwood, K., 30
Lipton, M., 20
Little, J. W., 22, 25, 31, 75–76, 82, 145
Lotan, R. A., 26, 141
Louis, K., 11, 13
Lucas, S. R., 8, 19–20, 136

Mac Iver, D. J., 13, 22, 97
Magnet high schools, 143
  in Baltimore, 4–5, 48–49
  enrollment trends, 5
Manno, B. V., 136
Manufacturing sector
  craft model of production, 7
  decline of, 9, 43–44
  mass production model of production, 7
Maryland Functional Tests, 59, 73, 97
Maryland State Department of Education (MSDE), 5, 12, 47
Mass production model of production, 7
Matthews, J., 9
McDill, E. L., 27, 149
McLaughlin, M. W., 82
McPartland, J. M., 21, 22, 27, 29
McQuillan, P. J., 141, 145
McTighe, J., 26
Miles, M., 11, 13
Mirel, J. F., 136–137, 138
Mood, A. M., 29
Morrison, W. F., 132
Multicultural curricula, 24
Multiple intelligences, 30–31
Muncey, D. E., 141, 145

Nathan, J., 136
National Association of Secondary School Principals, 14, 18, 31
National Center for Education and the Economy, 139
National Center for Education Statistics, 20, 26
National Commission on Excellence in Education, 20
National Commission on Teaching and America's Future, 31, 145
National Council of Teachers of Mathematics, 30
National Education Association, Committee of Ten on Secondary Studies, 7–8
National Education Commission on Time and Learning, 24
National Foundation for the Improvement of Education, 31, 145
National Science Foundation (NSF), 38
Nation at Risk, A, 5–6
Natriello, G., 19, 27
Neild, R., 4, 5, 26–27, 122
Neumann, A., 30, 141
New American High Schools Initiative, 14, 139
Newmann, F. M., 20, 22, 25, 26, 30
New Urban High Schools, 14, 139, 144–145
Ninth Grade Instructional Program, 37–38, 122–131
  curriculum of, 123–126, 129
  development and implementation of, 123–124
  field tests of, 127–130
  multiple tiers of teacher training and, 124, 127, 129
  professional development and, 124, 127, 129

Ninth Grade Success Academies
  balancing with whole-school reform, 92
  inter-academy conflicts and, 81–87
  nature of, 32–33
  at Patterson High School (Baltimore), 49–50, 55, 58, 66, 70, 81–87, 90, 91–92, 97, 122
  in Philadelphia schools, 116–117, 118, 119
  planning for, 102
  resources used by, 90
  in scaling-up process, 109–110, 116–117, 118, 119
  student promotion and, 88–89
  in Talent Development High Schools (TDHS) approach, 63
Nunnery, J., 141
Nussel, E., 13–14

Oakes, J., 8–9, 20, 27
Ogbu, J. U., 19
Olney High School (Philadelphia)
  planning process for, 114–115
  in scaling-up process, 106–109
Olson, L., 23
Once and Future School, The (Herbst), 135
O'Neil, J., 24
Open Society Institute, 140
Orfield, G., 12
Organizational facilitators, 39
Orr, M., 44–46, 59
Oxley, D., 18, 19

Pallas, A. M., 27, 30, 141
Partnerships, in Talent Development High Schools (TDHS) approach, 34–35, 94–95, 116–117, 118
Patterson High School (Baltimore), 15, 61–77, 81–99
  administrative staff decentralization, 52, 56
  background of restructuring program, 48–49
  Career Academies, 51–56, 81–87, 92
  effects of reforms in, 65–77
  eligibility for reconstitution, 47, 48
  emerging divisions in second year of TDHS program, 87–92
  expectations for change after school restructuring, 61–64
  Harlem Middle Park School model for reconstitution, 48–49
  Hyde plan model for reconstitution, 48, 50, 51
  implementation hurdles, 81–91
  lessons learned from, 92–96
  multiple academy model, 51–54
  Ninth Grade Success Academy, 49–50, 57
  partnership with Johns Hopkins Center for Social Organization of Schools, 50–51
  planning for school restructuring, 51–59, 103, 105, 142
  professional development and, 58
  reform plan, 48–51
  sustaining reform at, 96–98
  Twilight School, 50, 72–73, 88
Penn Towns, D., 22
Philadelphia, Pennsylvania. *See also* Edison High School (Philadelphia); Olney High School (Philadelphia); Strawberry Mansion High School (Philadelphia)
  analysis of 9th-grade repeaters, 5
  keystone provision in, 106–107
  Ninth Grade Instructional Program, 37–38, 122–131
  risk factors of high school students, 4
  scaling-up in, 106–109, 114–133
Philadelphia Education Collaborative, 141
Philadelphia Education Fund (PEF), 116–117, 118, 119, 128–129
Piore, M. J., 6–7
Planning for school restructuring, 146–147
  in Baltimore scale-up, 101–106

at Patterson High School (Baltimore), 51–59, 103, 105, 142
in Philadelphia scale-up, 114–117
Policy churn (Hess), 13
Pollack, J. M., 27
Poverty
in Baltimore, Maryland, 44–45
school climate and, 12
in urban areas, 10–11, 12–13, 139
Powell, A., 8–9, 11
Principals
importance of, 108–109
relationships between faculty members and, 108–109
successors to, 96, 97, 109–110
in Talent Development High Schools (TDHS) approach, 84–86, 89, 90–94, 108–109
Private schools, common core curriculum of, 21
Professional development, 21
new methods of, 31, 145
for Ninth Grade Instructional Program, 124, 127, 129
at Patterson High School (Baltimore), 58
in Philadelphia schools, 117
in Talent Development High Schools (TDHS), 31, 38–39

Queen, J. A., 25, 37

Raby, M., 23, 115
Racism, 8
Reconstitution of failing schools, in Baltimore, Maryland, 45, 46–47, 48, 50, 51, 92–94
Resnick, L. B., 23, 26, 30–31
Resources
in comprehensive high schools, 11
in Talent Development High Schools (TDHS) approach, 90, 95
Rettig, M. D., 25, 55
Rivkin, S. G., 12
Rock, D. A., 27
Roderick, M., 5, 26, 27
Rosenstock, L., 139, 144–145
Ross, S., 141
Ruiz-de-Velasco, J., 12
Rury, J. L., 12
Rusk, D., 10, 59

Sabel, C. F., 6–7
Sarason, S. B., 136
Saturday school, 34, 56
Scaling-up
in Baltimore, 101–106, 109–113, 127–128
defined, 100
fast-track schools in, 102–106, 109–113
Johns Hopkins/CRESPAR resources in, 101–102, 104, 105–106, 107, 110, 115
on-site facilitation in, 105–106, 120
in Philadelphia, 106–109, 114–133
Scheduling
block, 24–25, 36–37, 55–56, 66, 120–122
in "factory" model, 24
flexible, 84
Schmoke, Kurt, 45, 46
Schneider, B., 21
School climate
in comprehensive high schools, 12
data collection on, 65
effects of educational reform on, 67–70
expectations for change with TDHS approach, 62–63
in scaling-up process, 117–122
School organization, 29–30
academies in. *See* Career Academies; Ninth Grade Success Academies
centralized, 29
communal, 29–30
School Performance Index
defined, 97
effects of educational reform on, 73–75, 97

School size
  of comprehensive high schools, 18–19
  increase in, from educational reform, 148–149
School-to-career movement, 23
School-to-work movement, 23, 144–145
School to Work Opportunities Act (1994), 23
School-within-a-school concept, 17, 32–33, 35–36. *See also* Talent Development High Schools (TDHS) approach
  facilities changes and, 54–55
  at Harlem Park Middle School, 48–49
  at Patterson High School (Baltimore), 51–55
Schorr, Lisbeth, 100
Schulz, L., 132
Secondary education, 6–10. *See also* Comprehensive high schools; Talent Development High Schools (TDHS) approach
  first historical divide in, 7–8
  flexible specialization in, 7
  second historical divide in, 8–10
Second Industrial Divide, The (Piore and Sabel), 6–7
Secretary's Commission on Achieving Necessary Skills (SCANS), 23
Security officers, 69–70
Segregation, in comprehensive high schools, 12–13, 135
Segregation in schools, 135
Senge, P. M., 29
Siskin, L. S., 25
Site-based management, 46, 90
Sizer, Theodore R., 8–9, 19, 26
Slavin, R. E., 26, 149
Small learning communities (SLCs), 19. *See also* Career Academies; Ninth Grade Success Academies; Twilight School
  interdisciplinary teams and, 22, 32, 119
  in Talent Development High Schools (THDS), 32–33, 61–64
Smith, J. B., 18, 20, 21, 22, 30
Smith, J. L., 21
Smith, L., 141
Smrekar, C., 136
Smylie, M. A., 31
Snodgrass, D. M., 26
Soros, George, 140
Southern Regional Education Board, 139
Sparks, D., 31
Special education programs, 89, 91, 94, 96, 143–144
Spinning Wheels (Hess), 13
Standards
  in measuring school improvement, 136–138
  student promotion and, 88–89
Standards-based approach, 136–138
Steinbach, R., 30
Stern, D., 23, 115
Stevenson, H. W., 26
Stigler, J. W., 26
Stone, J., III, 23
Strawberry Mansion High School (Philadelphia), 15–16
  implementation process, 115–122, 132–133
  Ninth Grade Instructional Program, 122–131
  planning process for, 115
Stringfield, S., 6, 100, 141
Student achievement
  in comprehensive high schools, 11–12, 18
  data collection on, 65, 112
  effects of educational reform on, 73, 112
  expectations for change with TDHS approach, 64
  in School Performance Index, 97
Student attendance

in comprehensive high schools, 18
data collection on, 65, 110–111
effects of educational reform on, 70–71, 110–111
expectations for change with TDHS approach, 63–64
in scaling-up process, 117–122
in School Performance Index, 97
Student-centered approach, 26
Student promotion
data collection on, 65, 111
effects of educational reform on, 71–73, 88–89, 111, 120, 131
expectations for change with TDHS approach, 64
standards and, 88–89
Summer school, 34
Summer Training and Education Program (STEP), 27
Superintendent, turnover among urban, 13

Talent Development High Schools (TDHS) approach, 27–40. *See also* Edison High School (Philadelphia); Patterson High School (Baltimore); Strawberry Mansion High School (Philadelphia)
alternatives to, 139
in Baltimore, 43–77, 81–106, 109–113
blended instruction in, 36
block scheduling in, 36–37
Career Academies in. *See* Career Academies
challenges to creating, 15
cognition and learning in, 30–31
in combating anonymity, 32–35
in combating apathy, 35–37
contextual instruction in, 36
criticisms of comprehensive high schools and, 18–27, 28
described, 6, 14–15
effects of reforms based on, 65–77
expectations for change, 61–64
financial issues in, 90, 95
Freshman Seminar in, 33, 39
implementation hurdles, 81–92, 115–117, 147–148
interdisciplinary instruction in, 36
Ninth Grade Instructional Program. *See* Ninth Grade Instructional Program
Ninth Grade Success Academies. *See* Ninth Grade Success Academies
partnerships in, 34–35, 94–95, 116–117, 118
in Philadelphia, 106–109, 114–133
polarized leadership in, 90–92
professional development and, 31, 38–39
recovery opportunities in, 34
reform responses to criticisms of comprehensive high schools, 18–27, 28
research design for study of, 64–65
scaling-up efforts, 100–113, 114–133
school organization and, 29–30
small learning communities in, 32–33
special education in, 89, 91, 94, 96, 143–144
and strength in diversity, 37–38
support services for at-risk students in, 34
technical assistance and, 38–39
theoretical supports for, 29–31
transitions of students in, 37–38
Twilight School, 34, 50, 63, 72–73, 88, 120
upper grade advisors in, 33
Teacher teaming, 22, 32, 119, 145
Teaching methods, in comprehensive high schools, 25–26
Technical assistance, 38–39
Tesseract Group, Inc., 48
Thum, Y. M., 27
Title I programs, 95

Top-down administration, 91, 93, 94
Tracking, 8, 17, 19–21
common core curriculum versus, 20–21, 142–144
problems of, 20, 22–23, 135
Tracking Inequality (Lucas), 8
Transitions of students
in comprehensive high schools, 26–27
Freshman Seminar, 33, 39
in Talent Development High Schools, 33, 37–38
in Talent Development High Schools (TDHS) approach. *See also* Ninth Grade Instructional Program; Ninth Grade Success Academies
upper grades advisors, 33
Twilight School, 34
at Patterson High School (Baltimore), 50, 72–73, 88
in Philadelphia schools, 120
in Talent Development High Schools (TDHS) approach, 63
Tyack, D., 7

Union leaders, 107–108
U.S. Bureau of Labor Statistics, 9
U.S. Census Bureau, 10, 11, 44
U.S. Department of Education, 11, 14, 20, 26, 70, 139
University-based partners, 6, 15, 50–51, 90, 94, 98–99
University of Chicago School Mathematics Project, 38
University of Maryland System, 44, 97–98
Upper grades advisors, 33

Vanourek, G., 136

Wall-to-Wall Career Academies, 32, 33. *See also* Career Academies
Wehlage, G. G., 20, 22
Weinfeld, F. D., 29
"White flight," 10–11, 44
Whole-school restructuring models, 6, 17–18, 61–62, 92–94, 95, 96, 147. *See also* Talent Development High Schools (TDHS) approach
Wiggins, G., 26
Wilson, Bruce L., 118–122, 125–126, 132
Wirt, J. G., 23
Wraga, W. G., 7, 19

Yonezawa, S. S., 20
York, R. L., 29

About the Authors

Nettie E. Legters is an associate research scientist with the Johns Hopkins University Center for Social Organization of Schools, and associate director of the Talent Development High Schools (TDHS) program. She received her doctorate in sociology from Johns Hopkins University. Committed to translating research into policy and practice, Dr. Legters has worked closely with replication sites to guide planning and implementation of TDHS reforms. She is lead author of *Creating a Talent Development High School: The Planning Process,* co-author of the TDHS manual on *Creating a Ninth Grade Success Academy,* and has worked as an on-site organizational facilitator in several large, urban high schools. Her research and writings have focused on high school restructuring, comprehensive school reform, teachers' work, and equity in urban education. Her recent work addresses organizational change in high schools, the role of the organizational facilitator, and the effectiveness of different approaches to in-service professional development for teachers and administrators.

Robert Balfanz is an associate research scientist and associate director of the Talent Development High Schools program. Dr. Balfanz has 15 years experience in the research, development, design, and implementation of curricular and instructional reforms. A central focus of his research and development work is translating research findings into effective classroom interventions. His published works include *Everyday Mathematics* produced by the University of Chicago School Mathematics Project (UCSMP), which is currently used by over 2 million students nationwide. He leads the TDHS curriculum and instruction research and development team and also is co-developer of the TDHS Transition to Advanced Mathematics course. Dr. Balfanz has written widely on the implementation challenges faced by comprehensive school reform models and the characteristics of secondary schooling in large urban school districts. He received his Ph.D. in Education from the University of Chicago.

Will J. Jordan is currently a senior sociologist at The CNA Corporation in Alexandria, Virginia. During the production of this book he held the positions of associate research scientist and associate director of the Center for Social Organization of Schools at Johns Hopkins University. Dr. Jordan earned his Ph.D. in sociology and education at Teachers College, Columbia University. His research has focused upon various issues related to the education and social experiences of adolescents. Throughout his career, Dr. Jordan has maintained a particular interest in studying youth at risk of educational failure and creating policies and programs to improve the odds of their educational success.

James McPartland is professor of sociology and director of the Johns Hopkins University Center for Social Organization of Schools. He also is director of the Talent Development High Schools program. He received his doctorate in sociology from Johns Hopkins and spent his early research years in Washington, DC as co-author of the Coleman Report, *Equality of Educational Opportunities,* and as a contributor to the U.S. Commission on Civil Rights report *Racial Isolation in the Public Schools.* His work continues to emphasize effective schooling for students from poor and minority backgrounds with a current focus on high schools. In addition to his research, Dr. McPartland is active in restructuring high schools and serves on numerous national and regional groups studying and promoting high school reform.